ROCKS
MINERALS
& GEMS

ROCKS MINERALS & GEMS

Sean Callery and
Miranda Smith

SCHOLASTIC

Art director: Bryn Walls
Managing editor: Miranda Smith
Designer: David Ball
US editor: Stephanie Engel
Consultants:
Professor James D. Webster, American Museum
of Natural History, New York
Dr. Wendy Kirk, University College London
Dr. David Cook
Special photography taken at University College
London, Steetley Minerals, and Holts London
by Gary Ombler

ISBN 978-0-545-94719-0

22 21 20 19 18   23 24 25 26 27

Printed in China   38
First edition, August 2016

Scholastic is constantly working to lessen the
environmental impact of our manufacturing processes.
To view our industry-leading paper procurement policy,
visit www.scholastic.com/paperpolicy.
Scholastic Inc., 557 Broadway, New York, NY 10012.

Foreword **6**
Spotlight introductions **8**

MINERALS **14**

Mineral gallery 16
Copper **18**
Cuprite, the ruby crystal **20**
Malachite **22**
Graphite **24**
Platinum **26**
Iron **28**
Fool's gold **30**
Gold **32**
Silver **34**
Clay minerals **36**
Clay warriors **38**
Olivine **40**
Meteorite gallery 42
Feldspars **44**
Zircon **46**
Scheelite **48**
More minerals 50
Chromite **52**
Galena **54**
Galena and quartz **56**
Hematite **58**
Magnetite **60**
Metal minerals **62**
Chalcedony **64**
Borax **66**
Bauxite **68**
Fluorite **70**
Light and dark **72**
Calcite **74**
Calcite network **76**
Barite **78**
Sphalerite **80**
Cinnabar **82**
Arsenopyrite **84**
Arsenic mineral **86**

ROCKS 88

Igneous rock gallery 90
Granite 92
Basalt 94
Pegmatite 96
Volcanic wilderness 98
Tuff 100
Pumice 102
Obsidian 104
Obsidian band 106
Gabbro 108
Dolerite 109
Sedimentary rocks 110
Limestone 112
Time capsules 114
Chalk 116
Breccia 118
Shale 119
Fossil gallery 120
Sandstone 122
Sandstone canyon 124
Tufa 126
Rock salt 128
Rock gypsum 129
More sedimentary rocks 130
Coal 132
Underground reserves 134
Flint 136
Metamorphic rocks 138
Marble 140
Natural wonder 142
Schist 144
Gneiss 145
Quartzite 146
Fulgurite 147
Slate 148
Black slate pavement 150
Hornfels 152
Amphibolite 154
Eclogite 155

GEMS 156

Gem gallery 158
Garnet 160
Beryl 162
Emerald 164
Gem of a find 166
Aquamarine 168
Tourmaline 170
Gem-quality tourmaline 172
Agate 174
Quartz 176
Quartz in all its glory 178
Amethyst 180
Citrine 182
Opal 184
Precious stone 186
Topaz 188
More gems 190
Sapphire 192
Ruby 194
Diamond 196
Diamond crystal 198
Turquoise 200
Jade 202
Lapis lazuli 204
Jet 205
Pearl 206
Coral 207
Red beauty 208
Amber 210
Perfectly preserved 212

Glossary 214
Index 219
Acknowledgments 224

FOREWORD

Rocks and minerals are wonders of our world, and most are forged in natural furnaces miles below our feet. They form the land on which we walk, and provide the raw materials that allow us to live how we wish to live.

There is a kind of magic in the fact that these basic elements of our world—materials that we take completely for granted—are part of a story that began in incredible heat and pressure, below the shifting continents that push mountains up on Earth's crust. Take a simple curbstone—what a story it has: born in magma; blasted from a volcano; collected, ground up, and transformed into an unnoticed, everyday part of our world.

This book tells those stories, of how everything from railroad ballast rock to the most brilliant gems on a glittering royal crown has been part of our planet for billions of years. It tells us what these materials are made of, where they are found, and how we change them for use in industry, art, and science.

PROFESSOR JAMES D. WEBSTER

DEPARTMENT OF EARTH AND PLANETARY SCIENCES,
AMERICAN MUSEUM OF NATURAL HISTORY

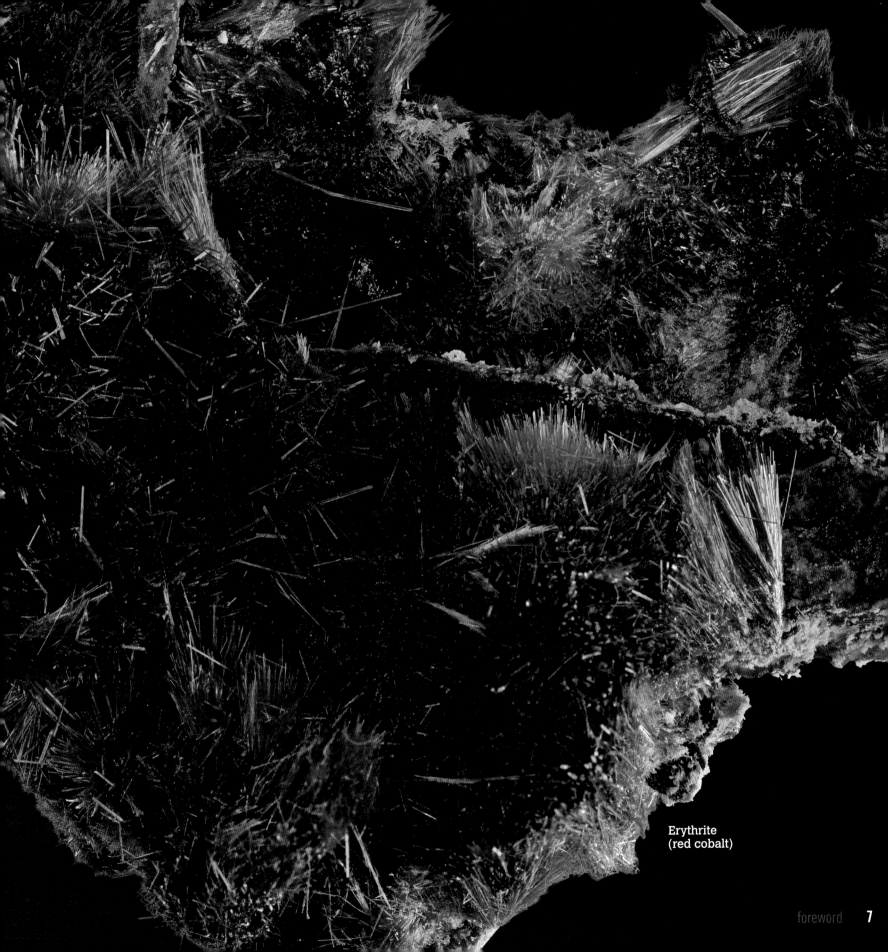

Erythrite
(red cobalt)

SPOTLIGHT | MINERALS

Minerals shape our world and touch our lives in hundreds of ways. These natural substances make up most of the world's rocks, but they are also found inside (and worn outside!) our bodies, as well as in the machines that we use and the buildings where we live.

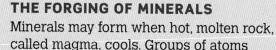

Kyanite

WHAT IS A MINERAL?

Minerals occur naturally. They are inorganic—they are not usually made from living things. They are solid at standard temperature and pressure—for example, water becomes a mineral only when it freezes into ice. Minerals have ordered internal structures. Their atoms are arranged in regular, repeated patterns. Their chemical compositions can be described by chemical formulas (for example, copper is Cu).

THE FORGING OF MINERALS

Minerals may form when hot, molten rock, called magma, cools. Groups of atoms come together to form crystals, which grow as more atoms attach themselves, like water drops freezing to make an icicle bigger. Some minerals are left behind when water evaporates or cools. Sometimes, new minerals form when existing minerals are altered chemically by air or oxygen-rich water. Other minerals may be created when older minerals are changed by pressure or heat in a process called recrystallization.

Minerals are found in the rock, sand, and soil, deep underground, and on our planet's surface. Their science is called mineralogy, and those who study them are called mineralogists.

MINERAL SAMPLES

Anglesite crystals
on galena

Hematite

Chalcedony

Stalagmitic barite

Native silver

Vivianite crystals
in a shell

Fluorite on quartz

Galena spheres
on marcasite

Calcite (stained
with hematite)

Red crystals of
realgar in matrix

SPOTLIGHT|ROCKS

We could not live without rocks—we would have nothing to stand on or build with! Rocks form the crust of Earth, which rests on a thick layer of hot rock that flows like glue. At incredibly high temperatures, new rock forms as magma rises to Earth's surface, where it cools to a solid and becomes anything from a mountain to a seabed.

Fossilized sea urchin

WHAT IS A ROCK?

Rocks change over millions of years, reappearing in different guises in a process called the rock cycle. There are three kinds of rock—igneous, sedimentary, and metamorphic.

IGNEOUS ROCK

This rock forms from hot, molten magma in Earth's crust. Some cools and hardens underground and is known as intrusive or plutonic rock, after Pluto, the Roman god of the underworld. But some magma rises, oozing through cracks and erupting as lava. This is extrusive or volcanic rock. Small blobs may cool to solids in hours, while large pools can take weeks.

SEDIMENTARY ROCK

Sedimentary rock is made up of rocks broken into grains by ice, wind, and water to form sediment. This sediment might be blown, washed, or carried by a glacier to a new site, where the grains are compressed to form a solid. Sandy sediments are held together by a natural cement that forms in water when the debris collects. The three types of sedimentary rock are clastic (formed by weathering rocks), chemical (formed from minerals that dissolved and separated), and organic (formed from animals and plant debris).

Biotite gneiss

Shale

METAMORPHIC ROCK

This rock is formed when rock or sediment is buried below the crust and exposed to extreme temperatures or crushed—sometimes both—but does not melt. This changes its chemical structure to make new minerals. There are two kinds of metamorphic rock. Foliated rocks show layering or banding of minerals that have recrystallized under pressure. Nonfoliated rocks are blocky in appearance and are not layered.

ROCK SAMPLES

Granite
(igneous)

Tektite
(igneous)

Green marble
(metamorphic)

Snowflake obsidian
(igneous)

Biotite schist
with almandine
(metamorphic)

Migmatite
(metamorphic)

Millet-seed
sandstone
(sedimentary)

Chert
(sedimentary)

Tufa
(sedimentary)

SPOTLIGHT|GEMS

Many gems look like ordinary stones before they are cut, but when they are cut and polished, their brilliance and luster are enhanced, allowing the gems to shine brightly. The bigger or more transparent the gem, the higher its value. Some gems are shaped into jewelry to glitter from rings and necklaces, and others blaze from crowns.

Rough diamond

HOW ARE GEMS MADE?

After a volcano has blasted out hot rock, gems may form when hot, mineral-bearing waters fill volcanic pipes. Gems also form from concentrated rare minerals in pegmatites, which are coarse granite or other igneous rocks with large crystals inside. Under enormous heat and pressure, even tiny amounts of certain elements can change the colors of the stones. For example, both rubies and sapphires are made from the mineral corundum—tiny traces of chromium create the red in a ruby, while different elements such as iron or titanium turn sapphires green and blue.

THE BEAUTY OF GEMS

Jewelers classify gems using the four Cs: clarity, color, cut, and carat. Gems can be completely clear, but most contain inclusions—little bits of minerals or fluids, hollow areas, or fractures. The color of a gemstone influences its value, as does how well the gem is cut. In ancient times, gems were weighed with the seeds of the carob tree. Today, the standard weight is measured in carats.

Citrine

Cut diamond

Watermelon tourmaline

Emerald

Turquoise

Ruby

Gemstones have been imitated throughout history. Many lesser stones, glass paste, and manufactured materials have been used to decorate people, statues, and places. However, nothing sparkles as much as or is more beautiful than a glittering diamond or ruby.

Zircon crystal in matrix

Tourmaline

Lapis lazuli

Green beryl

There are more than 5,000 types of minerals, but only about 30 are common in Earth's crust. Minerals form naturally in Earth from the elements—simple substances that are not easily broken down. Most minerals are compounds of 2 or more of the 118 known elements—although gold contains only a single element.

MINERALS

MINERAL GALLERY

Born in the ground, minerals appear in an array of exotic colors. Each is precious as a jewel because each has special characteristics—for example some dissolve in water while others can endure incredible heat or pressure. With their countless uses, minerals are the mainstay of our world.

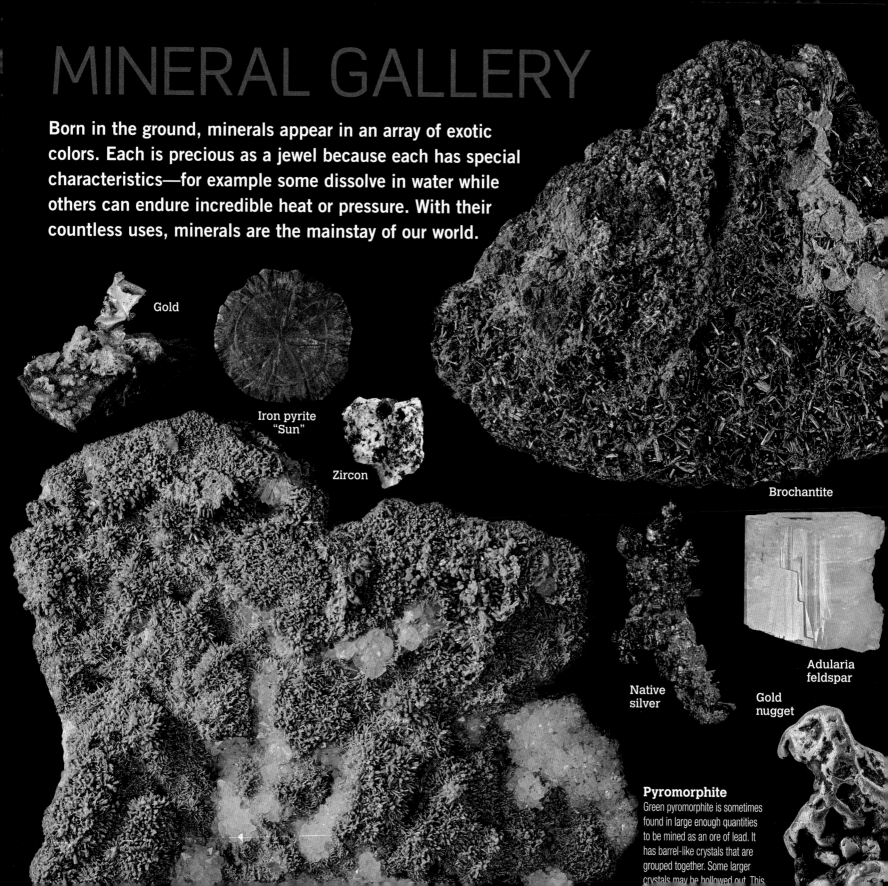

Gold

Iron pyrite "Sun"

Zircon

Brochantite

Native silver

Adularia feldspar

Gold nugget

Pyromorphite

Green pyromorphite is sometimes found in large enough quantities to be mined as an ore of lead. It has barrel-like crystals that are grouped together. Some larger crystals may be hollowed out. This

Cobalt on dolomite

Realgar (red) on calcite

Native copper

Graphite

Aragonite

Pyrite (yellow) on sphalerite (black)

Native copper

Barite

Calcite

Fluorite

Cinnabar on dolomite

Vanadinite (red) on goethite

Cerussite

Malachite

Chalcedony

Dioptase

Gypsum

COPPER

TRANSITION METAL

This mineral likes electricity and hates germs. It is a good electrical conductor, so our world is powered along copper wires. And it destroys harmful microbes, so many hospitals install copper surfaces. Probably the first metal used by humans, copper was prized by the Egyptians and mined by the Romans, and it makes fine tools, coins, and cooking pots.

COPPER SAMPLES

Native copper

Copper clustered in limonite

Copper containing cuprite, or copper oxide

Chalcopyrite, a copper iron sulfide mineral

Native copper

Group: native elements

Formula: Cu

Found in: volcanic basalt, often near sedimentary layers; hydrothermal zones; part of cement in conglomerates and sandstones

Main locations: Chile, US, Indonesia, Peru

Color: copper red to brown; light rose on fresh surface

Form: irregular masses; rare crystals are cubic or dodecahedral

Hardness: 2.5–3

Cleavage: none

Fracture: hackly, ductile, malleable

Luster: metallic

Streak: metallic copper red

Specific gravity: 8.9

Transparency: opaque

Crystal atlas: cubic

Uses: copper pipes to carry water; some superconductors; coins; electrical cables; telecommunication cables and electronics; cooking pots; tools; jewelry

Copper specimen

Copper is one of only a few metals that occur in nature in native form—that is, uncombined with other elements. The reddish-brown lumps of metal can be found buried in the ground, but other copper minerals such as chalcocite and cuprite are more economical to mine.

Blue-blooded octopus

In the freezing waters of the Southern Ocean, temperatures can drop to 28.8°F (–1.8°C), so the animals that live there have a difficult time transporting oxygen around their bodies. Antarctic octopuses have developed an ingenious solution to this problem: A copper-based protein in their systems called hemocyanin carries oxygen more efficiently—and makes their blood run blue.

Ankh symbol

In ancient Egypt, the ankh symbol denoted copper in the hieroglyphic writing system. It also symbolized eternal life.

BRONZE AGE CULTURE

For many cultures, the Bronze Age was the period during which the most advanced metalworking took place. It began in the Middle East around 3800 BCE, with the invention of bronze, produced by the smelting of copper (typically 90 percent) and tin (10 percent).

Ax head

This bronze ax head would have been bound with a leather strip to a wooden handle that slotted in between its raised sides. These axes were used as both tools and weapons.

Spearhead

In China, spearheads like this were coated in chromium oxide as early as the 8th century BCE. This helped prevent the copper from corroding.

Bronze mask

This magnificent bronze head depicts a ruler of the Akkadian Empire (2350–2150 BCE), near modern Baghdad, Iraq. The Akkadian court did much to promote innovative art, and this realistic portrayal was probably meant for display in a temple.

Sword hilt

This sword (ca. 700 BCE) was found in Bavaria, in southern Germany, where bronze and iron swords of the same type existed side by side. Many of the iron swords had bronze pommels. No bronze sword weighed more than 28 ounces (800 g), since otherwise it would have been too heavy to wield.

Shield

This bronze shield was found by archaeologists in Delphi, Greece. Groups of Greek warriors called hoplites formed seemingly impenetrable shield walls using similar round shields faced with bronze and strengthened with leather inner linings.

Cuprite, the ruby crystal

Sometimes known as "ruby copper," cuprite, or copper oxide, is very common in the upper layers of native copper deposits and even forms as a reddish coating over the copper itself. These transparent, bright red cubic and octahedral crystals are from the Copper Queen Mine in Bisbee, AZ. *Cuprite* comes from the Latin *cuprum*, which means "copper"; cuprite has a higher copper content than most other minerals. Very large cuprite crystals, often covered in a shiny green coating of malachite, are found in Namibia.

MALACHITE

COPPER CARBONATE

Deep down under the Earth's surface, circulating waters in a copper vein create something special—a green mineral that never fades. This mineral is named after the mallow, an edible plant prized by the ancient Greeks. Malachite is soft, so it is easy to shape and polish it into jewelry, or crush it to make the green pigment once cherished by artists.

MALACHITE SAMPLES

Malachite cross section with layering

Needlelike malachite

Malachite in weathered chalcopyrite

Malachite azurite conglomerate

Malachite in cuprite

Group: carbonates

Formula: $Cu_2CO_3(OH)_2$

Found in: sedimentary, metamorphic; usually near or banded with blue azurite

Main locations: Russia, Africa, Israel, England, France, US, Australia, China

Color: pale green to dark green; sometimes banded

Form: large crusts, bundles of long splinters, banded masses, botryoids, tufts of twinned needles and prisms; crystals are rare

Hardness: 3.5–4.0

Cleavage: perfect in one direction

Fracture: subconchoidal or uneven

Luster: vitreous, silky, or dull

Streak: pale green

Specific gravity: 3.9–4

Transparency: translucent

Crystal atlas: monoclinic

Uses: ornamental stones and carvings; tabletops; vases; jewelry; pigment; paints; minor copper ore

Green beauty

This stunning mineral is named after the mallow because the plant has bright green leaves. Malachite is a popular mineral because its softness allows it to take a high polish, and its green color does not fade over time or when exposed to light. It often forms in limestone, where it is usually found as stalactites or coatings on the surfaces of small underground cavities.

Jewelry
Semiprecious gems have always been popular, but malachite is liked for more than its beauty. Ancient Egyptians ground malachite for amulets to keep loved ones safe. In the Middle Ages, children wore malachite to protect them from witches

Painting with malachite
Malachite pigment was used to decorate the walls of tombs in ancient Egypt and was a popular paint in Europe during the 15th and 16th centuries. In this detail from *The Adoration of the Magi*, Perugino used malachite to paint the deeper green of the garments to contrast with the lighter green pigment of the grass.

Stalactite
Malachite is often found in stalactites and stalagmites. When these are sliced open and polished, they reveal dark and light green growth rings. This "bull's-eye" malachite is highly prized.

Mayan mask
This funeral mask of the Red Queen from Palenque, Mexico (600–700 CE), was constructed from some 220 mosaic pieces, mainly malachite. There are jade and obsidian inlays for her eyes.

Grand Kremlin Palace, Moscow
Russia had huge deposits of malachite that were mined in the Ural Mountains, and Russian czars used the mineral for ornaments and paneling in many of their palaces. The malachite foyer in the Kremlin Palace is named for its impressive malachite pillars.

GRAPHITE

CARBON

What links rockets, rackets, and oil? Graphite. This carbon cousin of diamonds is used in tennis equipment, in rocket nozzles, and to coat materials to keep out fire. It is made of tiny flakes that slide easily over each other, so it reduces friction in machinery when oil cannot be used. That's something to write home about—with a graphite-filled pencil!

Group: native elements

Formula: C

Found in: igneous and metamorphic, particularly schist and slate; pegmatites; hydrothermal veins

Main locations: China, India, Brazil, Canada, Turkey, Russia, Sri Lanka, Madagascar

Color: silver-gray to black

Form: distorted clusters or flaky plates, compact lumps, rare hexagonal crystals

Hardness: 1–2

Cleavage: basal, perfect

Fracture: uneven

Luster: metallic

Streak: black, shiny

Specific gravity: 1.9–2.3

Transparency: opaque

Crystal atlas: hexagonal

Uses: arc lamps; batteries; brake linings for cars; dry lubricant to reduce friction between mechanical components (e.g., brake shoes); rockets; fire doors; crucibles in steel, brass, and bronze industries; added to iron to increase carbon content in steel

Other names: plumbago, black lead, grafito, pencil ore

GRAPHITE SAMPLES

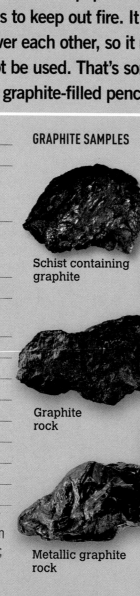

Schist containing graphite

Graphite rock

Metallic graphite rock

Graphite, handpiece

Natural graphite

Vein or lump graphite is the rarest and highest-quality form of natural graphite. It typically has a purity of 95–99 percent carbon. It is opaque, very soft, and easily scratched. It has the same chemical composition as a diamond (see pages 200–201) but a completely different molecular structure. In graphite, carbon atoms form sheets only one atom thick. They are not chemically bonded to one another very well so they cleave, or slide, over one another easily.

Pencil lead

The name *graphite* comes from *graphein,* which is ancient Greek for "to write." Graphite sticks wrapped in string came into widespread use at the end of the 16th century. Later, the graphite was inserted into hollowed-out wooden sticks, and the modern pencil was born.

GRAPHITE TECHNOLOGY

Graphite's unique properties are revolutionizing many new technologies. Many electric gadgets already contain graphite-filled batteries, reinforced carbon fibers have reduced weight in aerospace vehicles, and graphene chips may soon replace silicon in your laptop.

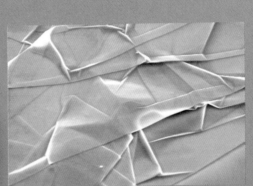

Fingerprint

Fingerprints on a light-colored surface are revealed by dusting them with graphite powder. The powder sticks to the moist prints, allowing them to be seen easily.

The miracle material

Graphene is a single layer of graphite only one atom thick. Because of its honeycomb structure, it is 100 times stronger than steel—it is said that it would take an elephant balanced on a pencil to break through a sheet of graphene the thickness of plastic wrap. In the future, it will be used for things such as flexible touch screens.

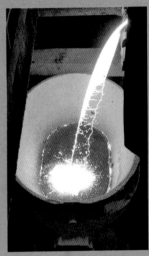

Heat resistance

Natural graphite is an excellent conductor of heat and electricity, and it is stable at high temperatures. It is often used to make the crucibles used for dealing with hot materials for industrial use (above), because it will not melt or disintegrate even under extreme conditions.

High performance

Today's cyclists love carbon fiber! It is the leader in performance road bike material. These bikes are three to four times lighter and stronger than other bikes, and much more comfortable.

Strength in the air

Many of today's state-of-the-art commercial aircraft have fuselages built with graphite epoxy. Made from carbon fibers embedded in an epoxy resin, this material is strong but only half the weight of aluminum.

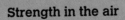

PLATINUM

TRANSITION METAL

The Spanish who conquered South America in the 16th century were baffled by the platinum they found in Colombia, because they could not melt it. Rarer and more valuable than gold, platinum is used in jewelry and for investment. It protects the planet (in catalytic converters to reduce pollution) and our bodies (in heart pacemakers and dental crowns).

Group: native elements, metallic elements

Formula: Pt

Found in: igneous, sedimentary

Main locations: South Africa (three-quarters of all platinum production), Russia, Zimbabwe, Canada, US, Colombia

Color: tin white, silver-gray, steel gray, dark gray

Form: nuggets, flakes, grains, rare cubic crystals

Hardness: 4–4.5

Cleavage: none

Fracture: hackly, ductile

Luster: metallic

Streak: silver-gray, shiny

Specific gravity: 14–19 because of dissolved iron and copper; 21.5 when pure

Transparency: opaque

Crystal atlas: cubic

Uses: jewelry; watches; coins, bars, and ingots for currency; oxygen sensors; spark plugs; catalytic converters in vehicles; missile nose cones; dentistry equipment and dental crowns (it is hypoallergenic); powerful magnets

PLATINUM SAMPLES

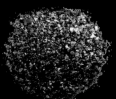

Platinum grains

Nugget of native platinum

Rough platinum nugget

A noble metal

Platinum is usually found as flakes or grains, and only very rarely as nuggets like this one. Known as a "noble metal," this is the rarest and heaviest of the precious metals. All the platinum ever mined—only about 135 tons annually—would fit in an average-size living room.

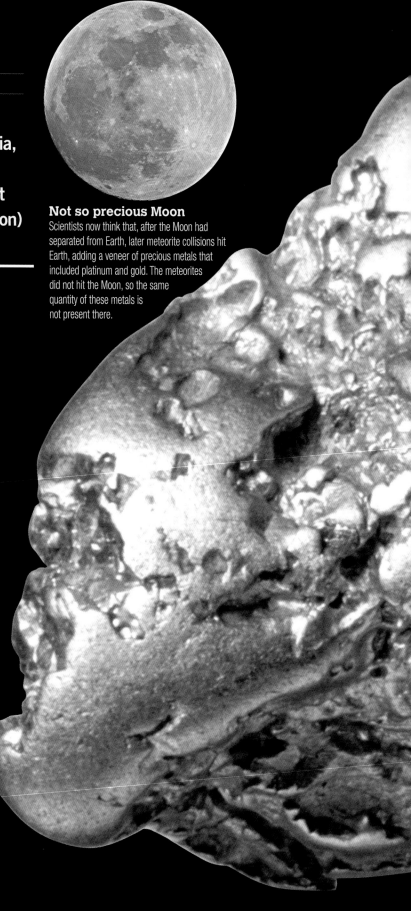

Not so precious Moon

Scientists now think that, after the Moon had separated from Earth, later meteorite collisions hit Earth, adding a veneer of precious metals that included platinum and gold. The meteorites did not hit the Moon, so the same quantity of these metals is not present there.

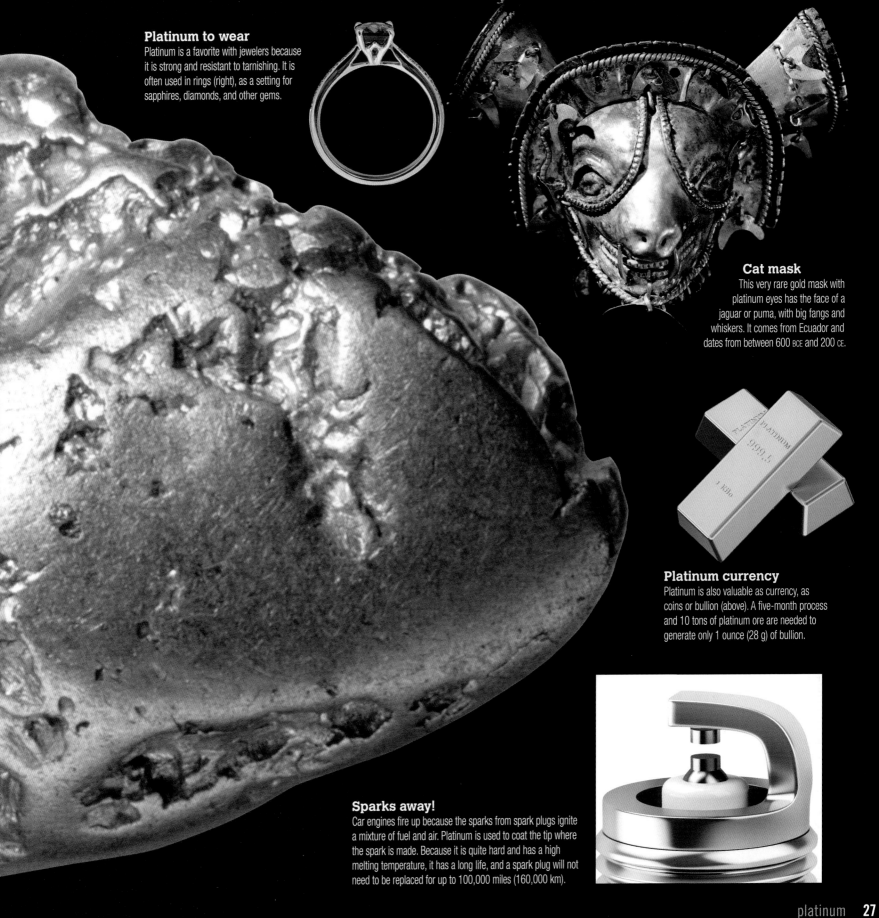

Platinum to wear

Platinum is a favorite with jewelers because it is strong and resistant to tarnishing. It is often used in rings (right), as a setting for sapphires, diamonds, and other gems.

Cat mask

This very rare gold mask with platinum eyes has the face of a jaguar or puma, with big fangs and whiskers. It comes from Ecuador and dates from between 600 BCE and 200 CE.

Platinum currency

Platinum is also valuable as currency, as coins or bullion (above). A five-month process and 10 tons of platinum ore are needed to generate only 1 ounce (28 g) of bullion.

Sparks away!

Car engines fire up because the sparks from spark plugs ignite a mixture of fuel and air. Platinum is used to coat the tip where the spark is made. Because it is quite hard and has a high melting temperature, it has a long life, and a spark plug will not need to be replaced for up to 100,000 miles (160,000 km).

IRON

METALS

Iron is so much part of our world—from Earth's core to inside our bodies—that it even has its own period in history: the Iron Age. This was when humans first heated ore to pour out molten metal that, when cooled, became a tough, hard material ideal for farming and fighting. Today, we use iron for buildings, toys, and—because it is magnetic—inside our computers.

IRON SAMPLES

Limonite iron ore

Iron pyrite

Magnetite, an iron oxide (see pp.60–61)

Hematite, an iron oxide (see pages 58–59)

Group: native elements; metallic elements

Formula: Fe

Found in: igneous; from meteors

Main locations: China, Australia, Brazil, India, Russia, Ukraine, South Africa, US, Iran, Canada, Venezuela, Sweden

Color: steel-gray to black

Form: masses; botryoids; nuggets

Hardness: 4

Cleavage: basal

Fracture: hackly

Luster: metallic

Streak: steel-gray

Specific gravity: 7.3–7.9

Transparency: opaque

Crystal atlas: cubic

Uses: steel from iron ore for lintels, cutlery, furniture, cooking pans; iron in our bodies helps oxygen travel; powerful magnets for use in computers; cell phones; medical equipment; toys; motors; wind turbines

There is enough **iron** on Earth to make **three new planets,** each with the same mass as **Mars**.

Iron ore

Iron is found in ores such as hematite and limonite. The metal makes up 5 percent of Earth's crust and most of its core. It can be stretched without breaking, is easily magnetized, and rusts quickly. When combined with carbon, it becomes steel.

BUILDING WITH IRON

Iron is a central part of our world. People first heated iron ores about 5,000 years ago, pouring out molten metal that cooled to a tough, hard material. Today, it is the most widely used metal on Earth.

Cast iron

Cast iron is iron that has been melted and poured into a mold to cool. Its advantage was that it was cheap and available. However, it had weaknesses in tension and bending, causing some disasters when structures collapsed.

Wrought iron

This is iron that has been heated and then worked with tools. It is primarily iron with small quantities of oxides. Highly malleable, it grows stronger the more it is worked. It has a much higher strength than cast iron and is often used for decorative elements because it is easy to shape. However, it was more expensive to produce than cast-iron.

Steel

Steel is an alloy of iron and other elements, primarily carbon. From 1870 (the Bessemer process for converting iron to steel was patented in 1856) cheap steels became available. Steel is very strong and one of the most common materials in construction and other industries. Both cast iron and wrought iron corrode easily, which gives coated steel a great advantage.

Fool's gold

Pyrite crystals have a brilliant metallic luster, attracting mineral hunters because their golden color stands out against rocky backgrounds. The mineral is called fool's gold because it is frequently mistaken for gold, despite the fact that, unlike gold, its crystals often have flat faces. Another difference is that pyrite is much harder than gold. It is an iron-rich mineral, and if struck against metal or a hard surface, it will create sparks. The name *pyrite* comes from the Greek *pyrite lithos*, which means "stone that strikes fire."

GOLD

TRANSITION METAL

Gold shines from pharaoh's tombs and astronaut's helmets. It is used to make our most special objects, from wedding rings to Olympic medals, and it is in the best scientific equipment because it does not tarnish quickly and conducts electricity well. Gold is so valuable that about a quarter of the world's supply is hidden away in bank vaults.

Group: native element

Formula: Au

Found in: igneous, sedimentary, metamorphic

Main locations: China, Australia, Russia, US, Canada, Peru, South Africa, Uzbekistan, Mexico, Ghana, Brazil

Colour: golden yellow to brass yellow

Form: octahedral, dodecahedral and cubic crystals; dendrites; nuggets; wires; flakes

Hardness: 2.5–3

Cleavage: none

Fracture: hackly

Lustre: metallic

Streak: golden yellow

Specific gravity: 15.5–19.3

Transparency: opaque

Crystal atlas: cubic

Uses: wires to conduct electricity; cell phones; computer memory chips; decorative gold leaf; gold bars; dentistry; Chinese medicine; modern medicine; spaceships and space visors to reflect infrared radiation; jewelry

GOLD SAMPLES

Thin plates of gold in quartz

Fine gold grains – (999.9 purity)

Crystallized gold

Gold panning

A prospector pans for gold in the Black Hills of South Dakota. This particular Gold Rush began in 1874. The gold the miners found was placer gold—loose gold pieces that were mixed with the rocks and other sediments in and around streams.

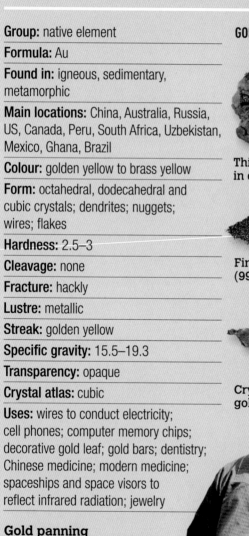

The **world's largest gold nugget**, the **Welcome Stranger**, was discovered in western **Victoria, Australia**, in 1869. It weighed over 157 lbs (**71 kg**).

Gold nugget

Nuggets are large masses of gold that are found in soil and stream beds. Gold is highly prized because it will shine for thousands of years without suffering from corrosion.

GOLD RUSHES

In the 19th century, fortune seekers from all over flocked to any site where there were newly discovered gold deposits. Whole families uprooted themselves and traveled vast distances to seek their fortunes. There were major gold rushes in the United States, Canada, New Zealand, Australia, South Africa, and South America.

1800
North Carolina

1828
Georgia

1848
Sutter's Mill, California By 1849, there were 80,000 "forty-niner" gold miners. By 1853, 250,000 had arrived.

1858
British Columbia, Canada

1851
Victoria, Australia Rich deposits were found in the Ballarat and Bendigo regions. The rush lasted until the early 1860s.

1861
Central Otago, New Zealand

1861
Eldorado Canyon, Nevada

1883
Tierra del Fuego, Chile and Argentina

1886
Transvaal, South Africa Two prospectors started the rush by finding gold in the district of Witwatersrand.

1896
Klondike, northwestern Canada

SILVER

TRANSITION METAL

If you want a metal that reflects light and conducts heat and electricity well, silver comes out on top. So it is used in mirrors, electronics, and industry, as well as for coins and jewelry. Why is it less valuable than gold? Because there's more of it, so it costs less, and it tarnishes in air.

SILVER SAMPLES

Elongated silver wires

Native silver

Native silver in matrix

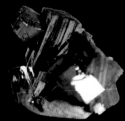

Crystals of pyrargyrite

Group: native elements

Formula: Ag

Found in: igneous, metamorphic; associated with ores such as tin, lead, copper, and gold

Main locations: Mexico, China, Peru, Australia, Russia, Bolivia, Chile, Poland, US, Argentina, Canada, Kazakhstan

Color: silver-white

Form: cubes, octahedrons, dodecahedrons, wires, masses, grains, scales

Hardness: 2.5–3

Cleavage: none

Fracture: hackly

Luster: metallic

Streak: silver-white, shiny

Specific gravity: 9.6–12.0

Transparency: opaque

Crystal atlas: cubic

Uses: defrosters in rear windows of cars; coins; photography; jewelry; batteries; dental fillings; electronics; silver-infused fabrics to prevent bacteria; control rods for nuclear reactors and other industrial applications; brazing and soldering; catalysts in chemical production

Early trade

The Mongol Empire flourished for 200 years, starting in the mid-1200s. Mongols traded using currency that they minted themselves. Their silver (above) and copper coins were minted in great numbers by special coin stamps on flattened pieces of metal.

Mining for silver

The first silver mines date back to 3000 BCE, in Anatolia (modern-day Turkey). The metal was used for jewelry and bartered for goods by traders. Today, silver-bearing ores are mined in open-pit methods or deep underground (right). Here, miners are drilling blast holes in a mine in Idaho.

Native silver

Most silver is extracted from silver ores such as pyrargyrite and galena (see pages 54–55), but the rarer native silver (left) is also mined in considerable amounts.

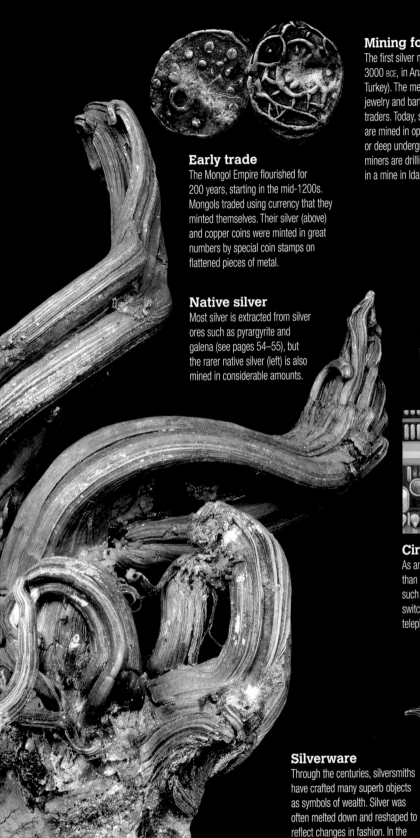

Value as currency

The rarity of silver has meant that the metal has been valued as currency for thousands of years. Today, many investors buy silver bars in order to build and preserve wealth.

Circuit board

As an excellent conductor of electricity—better than gold—silver is frequently used in electronics such as this circuit board. Silver membrane switches are used in buttons on televisions, telephones, computer keyboards, and microwaves.

Silverware

Through the centuries, silversmiths have crafted many superb objects as symbols of wealth. Silver was often melted down and reshaped to reflect changes in fashion. In the late 17th century, Louis XIV of France issued an edict that silver be brought to the mint for melting to replenish the state treasury.

Silver photography

The daguerreotype photographic process was invented by Louis-Jacques-Mandé Daguerre and introduced worldwide in 1839. Silver bromide and silver iodide were used in the photographic plates because they react to light and turn black.

CLAY MINERALS

SILICATE SHEETS

CLAY SAMPLES

Halloysite

Sepiolite

Kaolinite

Nacrite

Vermiculite

Some early civilizations lived in clay houses, drank from clay cups, and cooked in clay pots. The "clay age" continues to this day with clay being used in construction, for fertilizing, and even to make paper shiny. These tiny grains absorb water and become easy to shape, then dry as hard as rock—it's a very useful trick!

Group: silicates

Found: in association with limestones and sandstones in near-shore, shallow, and deepwater environments

Main locations: worldwide

Color: black, gray, white, off-white, brown, yellow, red, pink, dark blue, dark green

Form: plates, globular aggregates; almost plastic in appearance; rarely forms visible crystals

Hardness: 1–2.5

Cleavage: perfect

Fracture: uneven, splintery

Luster: greasy to dull; sometimes pearly

Streak: white, pale green to gray

Specific gravity: 2–3

Transparency: translucent to opaque

Crystal atlas: monoclinic, triclinic

Uses: bricks; tiles; porcelain, china and earthenware; pipes for drainage and sewage; construction; paper; plastics and rubber industries; fillers; medicines; lightweight aggregate in clay blocks for insulation; cement; pesticides; fuller's earth.

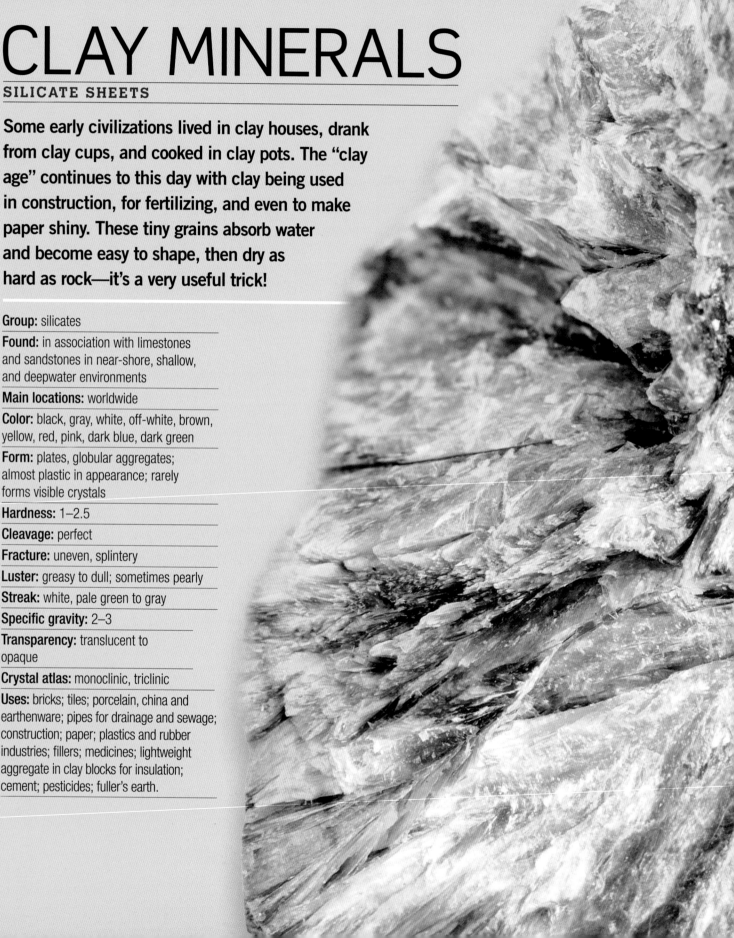

Adobe houses

Taos Pueblo in New Mexico was built at the end of the 13th century by Pueblo Native Americans. The multi-storeyed houses are made of sand, silt, and clay mixed with straw.

Chlorite

This green-tinged mineral is also known as clinochlore or clinkstone. It is often formed at high temperatures and pressures in metamorphic rocks during mountain-building events, but is found in sedimentary and igneous rocks as well.

CHINA AND CLAY

For more than 20,000 years, people have used clay—one of the most available of materials—to make everything from cups and dishes to extraordinary sculptures. However, it is the Chinese who have led the world in the potter's art, creating the finest bone china and porcelain.

Mayan pottery

Around 250 BCE, the Maya of Central America began to mold extras shapes onto everyday pottery. They made intricate human and animal forms, including this pecking bird.

Tang pottery horse

This elegant Chinese pottery horse dates from the Tang dynasty (618–907). It has three glazes called "sancai," meaning "three colors."

Delft blue

In 1602, merchants carried the first blue Chinese porcelain to the Netherlands. Until that time, Dutch earthenware tiles had been multi-colored. From 1640, the town of Delft produced blue on white tiles that became world-famous.

Porcelain

When certain clays, such as kaolinite, are heated to a very high temperature—2,200–2,600°F (1,200–1,400°C)—a fine china called porcelain is produced. It is very durable; pieces made in China 2,000 years ago have kept their colors and remained translucent.

Terra-cotta dish

When clay is fired it becomes terra-cotta, the Italian word for "baked earth." It is a material that has traditionally been used for everyday objects but also molded and decorated by artists through the ages. This painted and glazed terra-cotta dish is from the 1930s, and is in the Art Deco style.

Clay warriors

The Terra-Cotta Army has been a source of endless fascination since that moment in 1974 when farmers, digging a well near Xi'an in China, broke into a pit containing life-size terra-cotta soldiers. Further pits were uncovered, containing thousands more warriors, as well as weapons and horse-drawn chariots. This unique army was created to guard the tomb of the first emperor, Qin Shihuangdi, who united warring tribes in China more than 2,200 years ago and began the construction of the Great Wall of China.

OLIVINE

MAGNESIUM IRON SILICATE

Olivine is a group of minerals that form in cooling magma. It can really stand the heat, so it is used to create steam in saunas and form channels for molten steel in furnaces. In its rarest form, it is a gem called peridot. Tiny crystals of olivine were spotted floating through gas clouds at the birth of a star in 2011, and it has also been found on Mars.

Olivine pool
In Hawaii, olivine gems—known as peridots—are described as the tears of Pele, goddess of fire and volcanoes. Natural volcanic pools there are lined with olivine that glints green in the sunshine.

OLIVINE SAMPLES

Monticellite, olivine group

Olivine in matrix

Forsterite, olivine group

Gray-green olivine

Group: nesosilicates

Formula: $(Mg,Fe)_2SiO_4$

Found in: igneous, metamorphic, meteorites

Main locations: Norway, Japan, Spain, China, Brazil, Australia, Hawaii

Color: olive green, light green, dark green, yellow-brown, brown

Form: rounded grains, masses

Hardness: 6.5–7

Cleavage: usually poorly developed

Fracture: conchoidal

Luster: vitreous

Streak: white

Specific gravity: 3.2–4.3

Transparency: transparent to translucent

Crystal atlas: orthorhombic

Uses: jewelry (as peridot); bricks; heater rocks in saunas; refractory sand; added to blast furnaces to remove impurities from steel; magnesium ore; molds for molten metal (as olivine sand)

Other names: chrysolite

Olivine minerals
This group of minerals forms a major component of Earth's upper mantle. They are also found in the crust in some igneous rocks. Olivine takes its name from its color, which is usually olive green. Small and even microscopic grains are found worldwide, but large examples are rare.

Cut gemstone
Gem-quality olivine, known as peridot, can be cut and polished. Glittering peridot stones keep their shining color even under artificial light, so they are sometimes called "evening emeralds."

Egyptian gemstone
This 18th-dynasty talisman depicting a goddess, probably Hathor, holding the ankh sign of life is made from peridot. The talisman probably belonged to an olivine miner working on Zabargad Island (see below).

Zabargad Island
This island, where olivine was first found, was originally called Topazios by the ancient Egyptians—so peridot has often been mistakenly called topaz ever since. The mineral was mined only at night, because it could be more easily seen then.

Olivine "bomb"
Volcanoes that throw out magnesium- and iron-rich lava bombs when they erupt sometimes also carry nodules that are rich in olivine to the surface.

Olivine from space
Chondrite meteorites, like this one that fell in Mexico in 1969, make up 86 percent of all stony meteorites. They contain chondrules—small, round crystals of minerals including olivine and pyroxene.

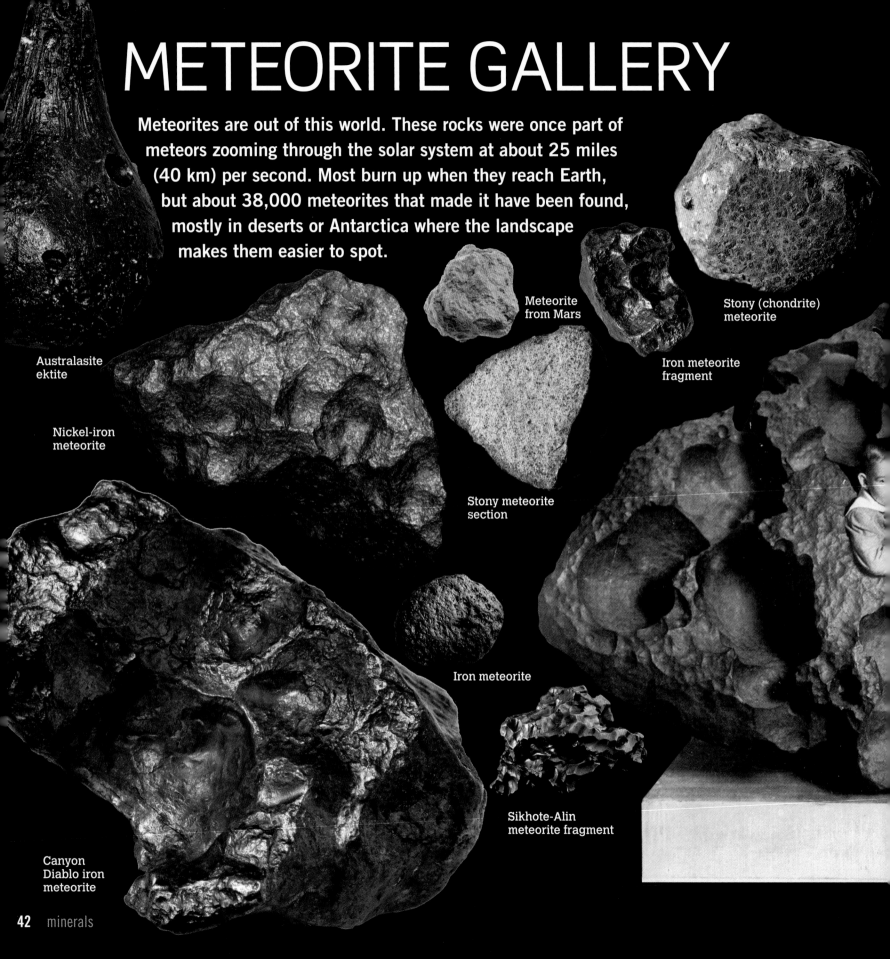

METEORITE GALLERY

Meteorites are out of this world. These rocks were once part of meteors zooming through the solar system at about 25 miles (40 km) per second. Most burn up when they reach Earth, but about 38,000 meteorites that made it have been found, mostly in deserts or Antarctica where the landscape makes them easier to spot.

Australasite ektite

Nickel-iron meteorite

Meteorite from Mars

Stony (chondrite) meteorite

Iron meteorite fragment

Stony meteorite section

Iron meteorite

Sikhote-Alin meteorite fragment

Canyon Diablo iron meteorite

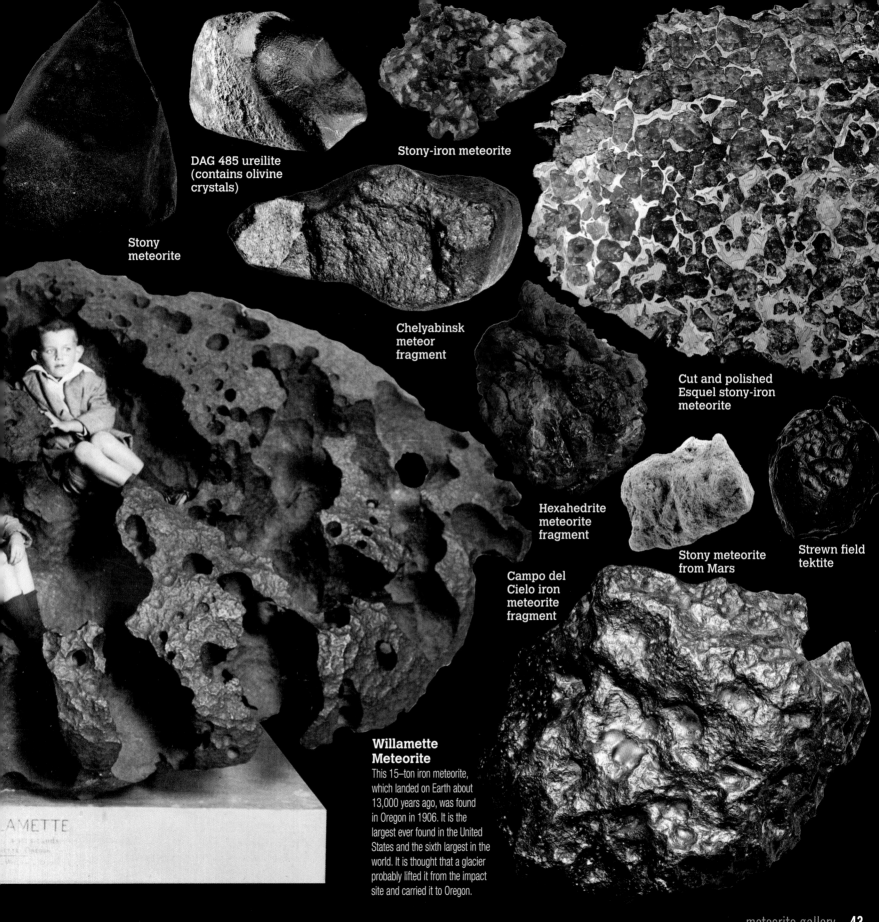

Stony
meteorite

DAG 485 ureilite
(contains olivine
crystals)

Stony-iron meteorite

Chelyabinsk
meteor
fragment

Cut and polished
Esquel stony-iron
meteorite

Hexahedrite
meteorite
fragment

Stony meteorite
from Mars

Strewn field
tektite

Campo del
Cielo iron
meteorite
fragment

**Willamette
Meteorite**

This 15–ton iron meteorite,
which landed on Earth about
13,000 years ago, was found
in Oregon in 1906. It is the
largest ever found in the United
States and the sixth largest in the
world. It is thought that a glacier
probably lifted it from the impact
site and carried it to Oregon.

AMETTE

FELDSPARS

ALUMINOSILICATE MINERALS

Feldspars are the unsung heroes of our everyday world—they are in our glass and pottery, insulation, and kitchen tiles, as well as many other things. But some feldspars have a glowing, magical quality that has captured our imaginations for thousands of years. These rock-forming minerals are found in two main forms: plagioclase and alkali.

Moonstones
The finest alkali feldspars, such as orthoclase and albite, can be cut and polished to produce semiprecious moonstones. In India, it is said that if people put them in their mouths during the full Moon, their futures will be revealed. The moonlike glow, known as adularescence, is caused by the reflection of light from the internal structure.

Sunstones
Gem feldspars that come from oligoclase are known in the gem trade as sunstones. In the early 1900s, Tiffany & Co. opened a sunstone mine in the United States and called the stones "plush diamonds." The colors are due to light reflecting off solid copper inclusions within feldspar.

Group: tectosilicates

Alkali feldspars: orthoclase, $KAlSi_3O_8$; sanidine, $KAlSi_3O_8$; microcline, $KAlSi_3O_8$; anorthoclase, $(NA,K)AlSi_3O_8$; albite, $NaAlSi_3O_8$

Plagioclase feldspars: albite, $NaAlSi_3O_8$; oligoclase, $(Na,Ca)Al_{1-2}Si_{3-2}O_8$; andesine, $(Na,Ca)Al_{1-2}Si_{3-2}O_8$; labradorite, $(Na,Ca)Al_{1-2}Si_{3-2}O_8$; bytownite, $(Ca,Na)Al_{1-2}Si_{3-2}O_8$; anorthite, $CaAl_2Si_2O_8$

Barium feldspars: celsian, $BaAl_2Si_2O_8$; hyalophane, $(K,Ba)Al(Si,Al)_3O_8$

Found in: igneous, sedimentary, metamorphic

Hardness: 6

Cleavage: alkali: perfect; plagioclase: good

Fracture: uneven or conchoidal, brittle

Luster: dull to vitreous

Streak: white

Specific gravity: 2.55–2.76

Transparency: translucent to opaque

Crystal atlas: alkali: monoclinic, triclinic; plagioclase: triclinic

Uses: porcelain, china, and earthenware; pottery glazes and enamels; glassmaking; clay; rubber; filler and extender in paints; in industry for alumina and alkali content; dating in archaeology; ceramic tiles; bonding agent in bonded abrasives (such as wheels or emery)

The **plagioclase** and **alkali feldspars** make up more than **60 percent** of Earth's crust.

Labradorite
The Inuit peoples of the Arctic claim that this mineral fell from the frozen fire of the aurora borealis. The shimmering, iridescent blues and golds certainly have a magical quality.

Martian meteorite
This polarized light micrograph is of a 0.001-inch-thin (0.03 mm) slice of DaG 489, a Martian meteorite rich in minerals. The olivine crystals appear beige, the pyroxene crystals are brown, and the feldspar crystals appear white.

PLAGIOCLASE SAMPLES

Mass of oligoclase

Glassy bytownite crystals in rock

Anorthite crystals in matrix

ALKALI SAMPLES

Orthoclase adularia crystal

Microcline crystals in rock

Sanidine crystal on trachyte

ZIRCON

ZIRCONIUM SILICATE

Zircon has a split personality. It can be a clear, diamondlike crystal, or light brown, but it turns many different colors when heated. This diversity is reflected in the variety of its uses, from sparkling as a gem on a crown to serving as an ore of the metal zirconium, which hardly ever corrodes and is used in power stations to protect us from nuclear radiation.

Fluorescent zircon
When it is viewed under ultraviolet light, zircon may fluoresce mustard yellow to orange. This helps greatly with identification by mineral collectors.

Group: nesosilicates

Formula: $ZrSiO_4$

Found in: igneous, sedimentary, metamorphic

Main locations: Australia, South Africa, China, Indonesia, Ukraine, India, Brazil, Canada, Norway, US

Color: colorless, blue, red, green, yellow, orange, brown, pink, purple, gray

Form: prisms to dipyramids; twinning is common

Hardness: 7.5

Cleavage: prismatic, indistinct

Fracture: conchoidal, very brittle

Luster: adamantine, vitreous, greasy

Streak: white

Specific gravity: 4.6–4.8

Transparency: transparent, translucent, occasionally opaque

Crystal atlas: tetragonal

Uses: ceramic glazes; whitener in porcelain tiles; bricks to line steel-making furnaces; foundries; surgical appliances; jewelry; one of the chief ores of zirconium

Other names: jacinth, Matura diamond, starlite, jargoon, hyacinth

ZIRCON SAMPLES

Oval red zircon brilliant

Round yellow zircon brilliant

Oval green zircon brilliant

Blue brilliant, heat-treated brown zircon

Never-changing
Zircon crystals exist in many colors and can reach large sizes. They are very hard, so they are resistant to change over billions of years. This means that they can help geologists date the rocks in which they are found, some of which are the oldest on Earth.

Almost as old as Earth

The oldest zircon mineral on Earth that has been dated so far is in the Jack Hills of Western Australia, seen here from space. It is in a metamorphosed sandstone conglomerate. Scientists found that the age of the zircon was 4.374 billion years, give or take 6 million years.

Zircon jewelry

This beautiful 18th-century silver necklace is set with topazes, zircons, and amethysts. Zircons come closer to resembling diamonds than any other natural gem. Both colorless and blue zircons are almost always produced by heat treatment.

Zirconium

Zircon is an important source of the soft, gray-white metal zirconium. Zirconium is used as a hardening agent in steel alloys, to encase nuclear fuel rods, and to make superconductive magnets.

Diamond-alike

Synthetic diamonds—diamonds that have been made by people rather than naturally formed—have been used in industry since the early 1950s. Today, gem quality synthetic diamonds are also available. Cubic zirconia, a form of zirconium dioxide, is one of the most popular diamond substitutes.

Sharp ceramic

Many kitchen knives today are made of an advanced hi-tech ceramic called zirconium oxide, also known as zirconia. It is extremely hard and wear-resistant.

SCHEELITE

CALCIUM TUNGSTATE

Scheelite looks like quartz, but miners can tell the minerals apart in the dark by shining an ultraviolet light, which makes scheelite glow blue. It's worth the hunt. Big scheelite crystals are highly prized as gems. Scheelite is also an important ore of the tough, heat-resistant metal tungsten, used on the outsides of rockets and the insides of lightbulbs.

Wolframite
Together with scheelite, wolframite is a major source of the metal tungsten. Wolframite's long, tabular crystals are very distinctive.

Group: tungstates

Formula: $CaWO_4$

Found in: igneous, metamorphic

Main locations: China, Russia, Canada, Austria, Bolivia, US, Australia, Scotland, England

Color: bright orange, yellow, brown, tan; sometimes white, purple, pink

Form: granular, columnar, or massive aggregates, small pyramidal crystals

Hardness: 4.5–5

Cleavage: good, parallel to pyramid

Fracture: conchoidal to uneven, brittle

Luster: adamantine or greasy

Streak: white to light yellow

Specific gravity: 5.9–6.1

Transparency: transparent to translucent

Crystal atlas: tetragonal

Uses: steel alloys and electric furnaces (as tungsten); imitation diamonds; scintillators; radium paint; laser mediums; filaments for electric lamps; drill bits; cutting tools

Scheelite crystal
This translucent orange crystal is named after the Swedish chemist Carl Wilhelm Scheele (1742–1786), who found that scheelite contains the metal tungsten. Good crystals of scheelite are rare, so it is sought after by collectors. The finest samples come from China.

Golden Point Mine, New Zealand

The fluorescence of scheelite under shortwave ultraviolet light is bright sky blue. Because this fluorescence is sometimes associated with native gold, it is used by people searching for gold deposits. This mine yielded about 880 tons of scheelite and 15,000 ounces (425,000 g) of gold in 40 years.

Powellite

This mineral is very similar to scheelite, although it is much rarer and contains molybdenum rather than tungsten. It forms crystals very like those of scheelite, but it fluoresces yellow. It is often found in quartz veins.

Tough metal

The metal tungsten has the highest melting point of all the elements except carbon, which makes it great for shaping metals, wood, plastics, and ceramics. The hard edges of chisels are made from tungsten.

Ready for launch

Saturn V is still the largest and most powerful expendable US launch vehicle ever built. It was used to launch the Apollo spacecraft between 1967 and 1973. Its rocket nozzles were made of strong, heat-resistant tungsten, and its combustion chamber was sprayed with tungsten carbide.

SCHEELITE SAMPLES

Scheelite crystals in muscovite

Scheelite crystals

White scheelite

Scheelite crystals on quartz

MORE MINERALS

Mineralogists study mineral crystal structure—crystals can be cubes, or have as many as 12 faces—as well as color, luster (appearance in light), and hardness (the toughest is diamond; the softest is talc). They also look at properties such as streak (color when ground down) and cleavage (how it splits).

Eisenkiesel quartz on hematite

Magnetite

Tourmaline with cleavelandite (white)

Hilgardite (orange) on boracite

Mica

Aragonite

Magnetite octahedron with hematite

Fluorite (purple) on quartz (orange)

Realgar

Calcite

Epidote

Wulfenite

Hematite (black), specularite, and quartz

Agate geode

Arsenopyrite

Scolecite

Dioptase

Gyrolite

Adamite

Boracite (green) with hilgardite (orange)

Fluorite

Stibnite
The metallic blue crystals of this mineral have the most extraordinary swordlike structure. Stibnite looks like silver, and for that reason it was once made into utensils for eating. However, it is poisonous, and needs to be handled with great care.

Cerussite

Amazonite

CHROMITE

IRON CHROMIUM OXIDE

Chromite makes the world more colorful—and tougher. Tiny amounts of the element chromium make rubies red and emeralds green, but it is also used to toughen the steel in our biggest buildings. China's Beijing National Stadium (the "Bird's Nest") is the world's largest steel structure. The outer shell was built with 42,000 tons of steel—16 miles (26 km) of it! The 24 main columns are each 1,000 tons.

Group: spinels

Formula: $FeCr_2O_4$

Found in: igneous, sedimentary, metamorphic, meteorites

Main locations: South Africa, Kazakhstan, India, Turkey, Russia, Oman, Brazil, Australia, Finland, Albania, Pakistan, China

Color: brown-black to green-black

Form: rounded grains, masses, nodules, rare octahedral crystals

Hardness: 5.5

Cleavage: none

Fracture: conchoidal to uneven

Luster: metallic to dull

Streak: dark brown

Specific gravity: 4.2–5.0

Transparency: opaque

Crystal atlas: cubic

Uses: to harden steel; glassmaking; in the manufacture of stainless steel; plating; bricks; anodizing aluminum for the aircraft industry; linings for blast furnaces

Other names: ferrous chromite

Chrome yellow

When Vincent van Gogh began to paint his famous sunflower paintings in 1888, his palette was dominated by a yellow pigment called lead chromate, or chrome yellow. This yellow-orange pigment was available in ready-made tubes of oil paint sent to him in Arles, France, by his brother in Paris.

CHROMITE SAMPLES

Chromite in serpentinite

Compact mass of chromite crystals

Light brown chromite nodule

Plagioclase containing chromite

Metallic rock

This mineral is a relatively hard, metallic black oxide composed of chromium, iron, and oxygen. It is the only ore of chromium, which is used for many metal, chemical, and manufactured products.

Building with chromite

The chromium extracted from chromite is used in the manufacture of steel because of its hardness and chemical resistance. The steel then becomes the backbone of structures such as this modern sculpture and skyscraper in Yokohama, Japan.

Chrome motorcycle

Chrome is resistant to corrosion and easy to clean—and it gleams! Many people want to own chrome objects such as this motorcycle. Chrome plating is a technique that uses electrolysis to bind a thin layer of chromium onto a motorcycle's different parts to give the desired shiny finish.

Chromium

Chromium, extracted from chromite, is a hard and brittle metal that is very resistant to rust. Rubies and emeralds owe their colors to chromium compounds, and potassium dichromate is used in the tanning of leather.

Crocoite

Crystals of the mineral crocoite, or lead chromate, are very fragile. Possibly one of the most beautiful minerals, it has a vibrant, flame-red color as a result of the chromium in its structure. It was first discovered in 1766 in the Ural Mountains of Russia. Larger and more brilliant crystals were later found on the island of Tasmania.

GALENA

LEAD SULFIDE

Black kohl extracted from crushed galena was the earliest eyeliner, worn by pharaohs and nobles across the ancient world, who thought it was magical. But galena's beauty has a dark side. For thousands of years, it has been the major source of lead, a common metal and a deadly poison.

Group: sulfides

Formula: PbS

Found in: igneous, sedimentary, metamorphic

Main locations: France, Romania, England, Germany, Bulgaria, Mexico, US

Color: lead gray, silver, with metallic sheen

Form: cubes, cubooctahedrons

Hardness: 2.5

Cleavage: perfect cubic, often breaking into smaller cubes when hit

Fracture: subconchoidal

Luster: metallic

Streak: lead gray

Specific gravity: 7.2–7.6

Transparency: opaque

Crystal atlas: cubic

Uses: main ore of lead; extracted lead for batteries, sheets, and shot; extracted silver; green glazes for pottery; radiation shields around nuclear reactors and X-ray equipment; natural semiconductors

Other names: lead glance, potter's ore

Metallic mineral
Galena is easily identified by its cube-shaped or octahedral (eight-faced) crystals. In addition to lead, galena often contains silver, zinc, copper, and arsenic. Argentiferous galenas can contain significant amounts of silver—most of Australia's mined silver is produced from this mineral.

Snowing metal

Beneath the thick clouds that cover the planet Venus, high mountains are covered with what looks like snow. But the average temperature on Venus is 867°F (464°C), and the "snow" is made up of heavy metals, mainly galena and bismuthinite (bismuth sulfide).

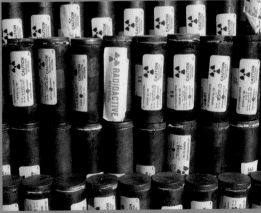

Early radio

A crystal radio set (above) was an early radio receiver that did not need a power source other than radio waves. The name came from the main component, the crystal detector, made from a piece of galena.

Modern power

You would go nowhere in a car without a lead-acid battery to supply power to start the engine. Smelted galena provides the lead for the batteries that power our lives in the 21st century.

Roman lead pipes

Ancient Romans smelted galena to release the lead and silver inside. They used the lead to line their aqueducts and to form pipes to carry water (above). They did not realize that it was poisonous.

GALENA SAMPLES

Basic cube form

Raw ore

Gray galena cubes

Galena spheres on marcasite

Anglesite crystals on galena

Mining town

Galena is the oldest mining town in Kansas. The existence of lead in the area had long been known to local Native Americans, but two young white men found quantities of galena there in 1877, and the town and its mining industry were born.

GALENA US 66

Medically radioactive

These lead canisters contain radioactive xenon, which is used in medical imaging. It is used in hospitals for SPECT (single photon emission computed tomography) scans and MRIs (magnetic resonance imaging). The lead prevents any harmful radioactivity from escaping.

Galena and quartz

Here, large white quartz crystals (see pages 176–177) are growing on a mass of dense, dark grey crystals of galena. Galena is one of the most abundant of the sulfide minerals, and it is often found with quartz in hydrothermal veins in rock. Hot magma heats water in the surrounding rock. The water dissolves materials from the rock and carries them to new locations. If the temperature, pressure, or oxygen content of the water changes, hydrothermal veins of new minerals such as galena, quartz, and sphalerite are formed.

HEMATITE

IRON OXIDE

Is there life on Mars? Maybe. Is there hematite on Mars? Definitely, and it gives the surface of Mars its red color. Early humans used hematite for its color, crushing it to make red chalk. A lump of this mineral is really heavy. It weighs more than five times the same volume of water, because its main ingredient is iron (see pages 28–29).

(see pages 28–29)

HEMATITE SAMPLES

Hematite mass from a vein

Hematite mass

Eisenkiesel quartz on hematite

Oolitic hematite

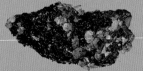

Specular aggregate of hematite

Black hematite with quartz

Group: oxides

Formula: Fe_2O_3

Found in: igneous, sedimentary, metamorphic

Main locations: US, Brazil, Venezuela, Canada, China, Australia, India, Russia, Ukraine, South Africa, Switzerland, England

Color: black, steel gray, red, red-brown

Form: thin plates, bundles of plates, masses, botryoids

Hardness: 5–6

Cleavage: none

Fracture: uneven

Luster: metallic to dull

Streak: red to red-brown

Specific gravity: 4.9–5.3

Transparency: opaque

Crystal atlas: trigonal

Uses: iron ore; gemstones (as cabochons); X-ray radiation shielding; processing of coal and other mineral material; compounds known as "red rouge" and "jeweler's rouge" to polish brass and other soft metals

Other names: red iron ore, kidney ore, specularite

Hematite ore
This beautiful iron-based mineral is one of the most important ore minerals of the metal iron. It colors the rocks we see. It gets its name from the Greek word *haima*, which means "blood."

The red planet
The NASA spacecraft *Mars Odyssey* found hematite on Mars in 2001. It is one of the most abundant minerals in the rocks and soils on the surface, so it gives the landscape the reddish-brown color that we see in the night sky. There is also gray hematite on Mars, which has raised the possibility that there were once hot springs on the planet.

Babylonian cylinder
In Babylonia (now Iraq), starting in 3500 BCE, cylinder seals were used to commemorate events, worn as amulets, and given as gifts. A cylinder was made from hematite (above left) or another semiprecious stone, and the picture story that it depicted was rolled onto wet clay.

Painting and drawing
When crushed, hematite makes an excellent paint that has been used by many civilizations. Prehistoric people used it for cave paintings, like this one from Tassili n'Ajjer in Algeria, and ancient Egyptians painted temple walls and tombs with it. It was also the principal coloring agent in the red ocher pigment popular with many Renaissance artists.

Hardworking mineral
Hematite is a hard mineral that is difficult to carve and can chip. However, it makes sharp and long-lasting images, so it is very useful for tasks such as sealing important documents. These hematite seals (left) date from 5150 BCE and were excavated from a prehistoric site in Syria.

hematite **59**

MAGNETITE
IRON OXIDE

Magnetite hangs with the tough guys—it is used to make iron (see pages 28–29), and it is added to concrete for strength and to block radiation. It is the most strongly magnetic of all the minerals. There is a legend that it is named after a shepherd, Magnes, in northern Greece, who discovered its magnetic properties when the iron nails in his shoes stuck to the rock.

MAGNETITE SAMPLES

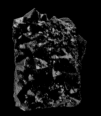

Black magnetite crystals

Gray speckled magnetite

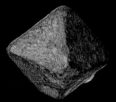

Octahedral oxidized magnetite with hematite

OTHER MAGNETIC MINERAL SAMPLES

Pyrrhotite, an iron sulfide mineral

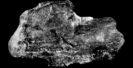

Columbite, an oxide of iron, manganese, and niobium

Group: oxides

Formula: Fe_3O_4

Found in: igneous, metamorphic; some sedimentary; hydrothermal deposits

Main locations: Scandinavia (especially Sweden), Switzerland, Russia, Bolivia, US, South Africa, Italy

Color: dark gray to black

Form: octahedral (and, less commonly, dodecahedral) crystals, crusts, dendrites

Hardness: 5.5–6.5

Cleavage: none

Fracture: subconchoidal to uneven

Luster: metallic to dull

Streak: black

Specific gravity: 4.9–5.2

Transparency: opaque

Crystal atlas: cubic

Uses: iron ore, used mainly in steel industry; abrasives (emery is a natural mixture of mainly corundum and magnetite); mineral collections; micronutrient in fertilizers; toner in electrophotography; pigment in paints; aggregate in concrete

Other names: lodestone

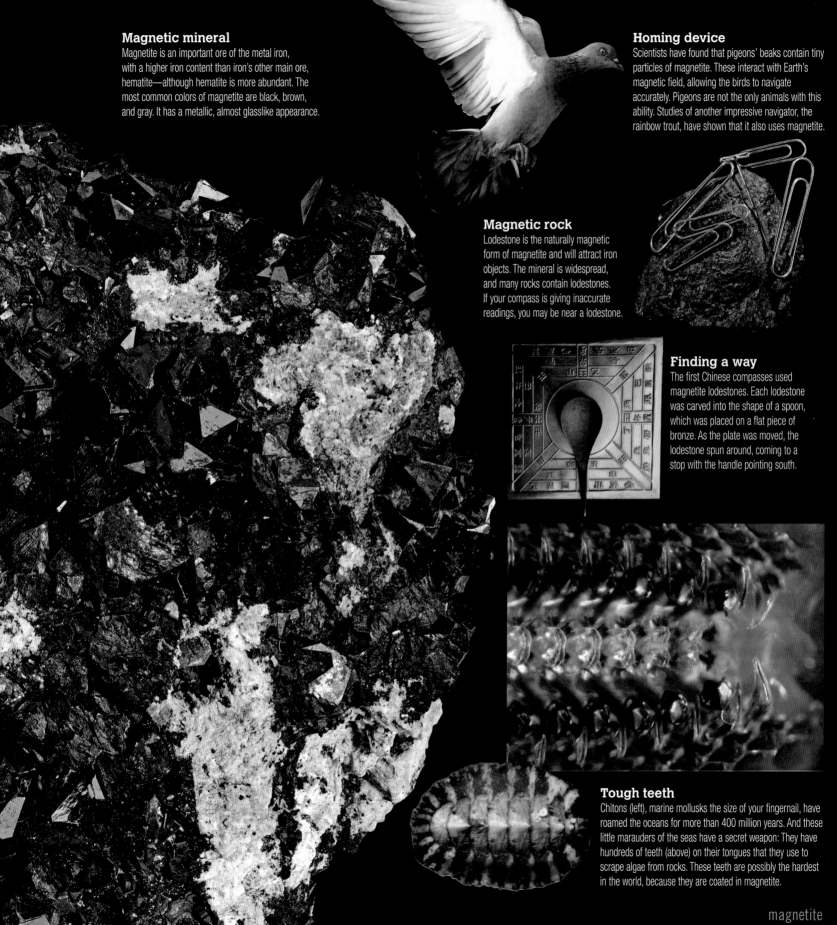

Magnetic mineral

Magnetite is an important ore of the metal iron, with a higher iron content than iron's other main ore, hematite—although hematite is more abundant. The most common colors of magnetite are black, brown, and gray. It has a metallic, almost glasslike appearance.

Homing device

Scientists have found that pigeons' beaks contain tiny particles of magnetite. These interact with Earth's magnetic field, allowing the birds to navigate accurately. Pigeons are not the only animals with this ability. Studies of another impressive navigator, the rainbow trout, have shown that it also uses magnetite.

Magnetic rock

Lodestone is the naturally magnetic form of magnetite and will attract iron objects. The mineral is widespread, and many rocks contain lodestones. If your compass is giving inaccurate readings, you may be near a lodestone.

Finding a way

The first Chinese compasses used magnetite lodestones. Each lodestone was carved into the shape of a spoon, which was placed on a flat piece of bronze. As the plate was moved, the lodestone spun around, coming to a stop with the handle pointing south.

Tough teeth

Chitons (left), marine mollusks the size of your fingernail, have roamed the oceans for more than 400 million years. And these little marauders of the seas have a secret weapon: They have hundreds of teeth (above) on their tongues that they use to scrape algae from rocks. These teeth are possibly the hardest in the world, because they are coated in magnetite.

Metal minerals

The sharp-edged, typically octahedral crystals are magnetite, while the reddish-brown crystals are the mineral rutile. This sample was found in rock in the Swiss Alps. Magnetite is an important ore of iron and is the only mineral that is a natural magnet, so small iron particles are often found clinging to its surface. Rutile takes its name from the Latin *rutilis*, which means "red" or "glowing." It is a major ore of the metal titanium, which is used for high-tech alloys because it is lightweight, resistant to rust, and very strong.

CHALCEDONY

MICROCRYSTALLINE QUARTZ

Chalcedony is the chameleon mineral, because it comes in so many colors. It is a variety of quartz made of microscopic crystals that are very hard and can be polished until they almost seem to glow. Its many forms include black and white onyx, orange carnelian, brown-banded agate, and deep red jasper.

Chalcedony
This fine-grained variety of quartz forms when silica-rich waters pass through cavities and cracks in rocks. It is white when it is pure, but trace elements give it a wide variety of colors. If it has strong banding, it is called agate.

CHALCEDONY SAMPLES

Chalcedony

Carnelian

Botryoidal chalcedony

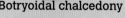
Jasper

Group: tectosilicates

Formula: SiO_2

Found in: particularly igneous; also sedimentary, metamorphic

Main locations: US, Uruguay, India, Madagascar, Mexico, Brazil, Africa, Germany, England, Russia, Australia

Color: white, colorless, gray, blue, red, brown, green, black, multicolored (due to traces of impurities)

Form: compact form of silica, microcrystals, masses, stalactites, linings of geodes; often banded, nodular

Hardness: 6.5–7

Cleavage: none

Fracture: conchoidal, subconchoidal

Luster: vitreous, waxy, or dull

Streak: white

Specific gravity: 2.6–2.7

Transparency: translucent to opaque

Crystal atlas: trigonal, monoclinic

Uses: gemstones; carvings; ornaments

Thin section of agate
Agate is probably the best-known form of chalcedony. It has many different varieties, all of which have distinctive patterns and bright colors. This polarized light micrograph of a thin section of agate shows how its colors are arranged in distinct zones.

Ammonite fossil

Petrification is a process in which original organic material is converted into a fossil, and the spaces are filled with minerals. Chalcedony is one of the minerals found in petrified fossils like ammonites (right), wood, and dinosaur bones.

Tigereye

This quartz crystal is a popular semiprecious stone. Quartz has replaced fibers of crocidolite, causing yellow and brown stripes. The stone is linked to the tiger, the king of beasts in Eastern mythology and is associated with courage and power.

Mexican knife

This sacrificial Aztec knife, dating from the 15th or 16th century, has a sharp chalcedony blade. The handle is carved from a single piece of wood to look like a crouching man dressed as an eagle warrior.

Rock rose

This sample, from Minas Gerais, Brazil, is an example of rose chalcedony. The name comes from the rounded shapes that resemble petals. The roses are often coated with sparkling crystals. This kind of chalcedony is also sometimes called concha or snake agate.

BORAX

SODIUM TETRABORATE

Borax stops grime and crime! The boron in these soft crystals, left behind when salty lakes dry out, is added to detergents and bulletproof vests. It even makes it into space in rocket heat shields.

Group: borates

Formula: $Na_2B_4O_5(OH)_4 \bullet 8H_2O$

Found in: sedimentary

Main locations: US, China, Turkey, Italy, Chile, Argentina

Color: colorless, white, light gray; light tints of blue, yellow, or green

Form: crystals, striations, encrustations, generally large crystals that are well-formed

Hardness: 2–2.5

Cleavage: perfect, imperfect

Fracture: conchoidal to earthy

Luster: vitreous to dull

Streak: white

Specific gravity: 1.7

Transparency: transparent to translucent

Crystal atlas: prismatic, monoclinic, sometimes twinned

Uses: disinfectants; detergents; water softeners; deodorizers; fungicides; herbicides; ceramic and glass manufacturing; coated paper; flame retardants; teeth-whitening products; mouthwash; bead testing (determining the presence of particular metals in a substance)

Tincalconite
Most borax loses water in its structure if it is stored somewhere dry. Although tincalconite is sometimes found in a natural state, it is most often the result of borax losing water, as with this sample. Tincalconite is known as "jewelers' borax."

Crystal garden

All you need is the detergent borax (see below) and a little hot water to create the most amazing crystals. As it cools down, borax forms crystals that can be made to cling to different materials and form different shapes. You can make crystal snowflakes, or a whole crystal garden complete with flowers. Always have an adult to help you.

BORATE SAMPLES

Ulexite, also known as television stone

Bulletproof borax

Boraz is an important ore of boron. Scientists have combined carbon and boron to create tough boron carbide. Thick ceramic plates of boron carbide are used in bulletproof vests, to protect tanks, and for heat shields on spacecraft.

Colemanite, a calcium borate hydroxide

Cleaning up

Many different forms of borate are used to produce laundry products. Borax is added to soften water.

20 MULE TEAM
ALL NATURAL SINCE 1891
BORAX
DETERGENT BOOSTER
& Multi-Purpose Household Cleaner
Removes Stains • Neutralizes Odors

Boracite, a magnesium borate chloride

20-mule team

Borax was mined in the United States after its discovery in the dry salt lakes of Death Valley, CA, in 1883. Teams of 20 mules were used to pull the wagons from the mines. The name 20 Mule Team Borax was later adopted for the detergent (above left).

Kernite, a principle ore of boron

Controlling nuclear reactors

To control the energy released in a nuclear reactor, movable control rods are placed between the fuel rods. Many control rods are made of boron, because it is excellent at absorbing neutrons and thus controlling the rate of a nuclear reaction.

borax

BAUXITE

ALUMINUM HYDROXIDE

Bauxite is named after Les Baux, the French town where it was first discovered in 1821. The name is the easy part—bauxite is made up of multiple minerals (mostly gibbsite, diaspore, and boehmite) that remain when certain rocks are chemically weathered in tropical conditions. Bauxite is the main source of the strong, lightweight metal aluminum.

Group: hydroxides

Formula: $Al(OH)_3$, with possible additional Al and (OH)

Found in: igneous, sedimentary

Main locations: Australia, China, Brazil, India, Guinea, Jamaica, Russia, Africa

Color: white, gray; sometimes yellow, orange-red, pink, brown

Form: spherical and claylike masses, botryoids, nodules

Hardness: 1–3

Cleavage: none

Fracture: earthy

Luster: dull

Streak: usually white

Specific gravity: 2.0–2.6

Transparency: opaque

Crystal atlas: monoclinic

Uses: oil, gas and steel industries; industrial abrasives; beverage cans; medicine packs; vehicles for transport; building construction; makeup; cement; water purification; as aluminum: wires, paints, alloys, furnace linings, ornaments

BAUXITE SAMPLES

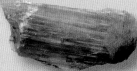
Rough diaspore

Gibbsite

Pisolitic bauxite

Bauxite nodules

Bauxite rock
Aluminum oxides vary considerably depending on their makeup. Bauxite rock is often claylike in appearance and can be quite soft. It is almost always found near Earth's surface, so it is relatively easy to mine.

At state dinners, Napoleon III of France served food to his most honored guests on **aluminum plates**; rank-and-file guests ate their food from **gold and silver dishes.**

ALUMINUM

Bauxite is almost the only ore of aluminum and the most abundant metal on Earth. Bauxite is a mixture of gibbsite, boehmite, and diaspore, which are the basic raw materials for aluminum production. Bauxite is also known as "solid electricity" because of the amount of power needed to separate out the metal.

Fireworks
Metals are used in fireworks to control their temperatures. They also burn very brightly and can change a firework's color. The brightest starbursts are fueled by aluminum.

Sputnik 1
On October 4, 1957, the Soviet Union (now Russia) launched Sputnik 1 into space. This was Earth's first artificial satellite. The pressurized sphere had a polished, 0.04-inch-thick (1 mm) heat shield made of aluminum-magnesium-titanium alloy.

Metal can
Aluminum is very much a part of our everyday lives. It is the second-most widely used metal; every ton of aluminum that we recycle saves up to 3 tons of bauxite.

Foil blanket
Aluminum is very lightweight and strong, and it is also reflective. This means that it makes excellent emergency blankets that can keep people warm at accident scenes. The blanket reflects heat back in toward the wearer.

bauxite **69**

FLUORITE
CALCIUM FLUORIDE

Fluorite is a show-off. Not only does it come in a wide range of colors, earning it the reputation of the most colorful mineral in the world, but some varieties even glow in ultraviolet light (which is where the word *fluorescence* comes from). It is used to make jewelry, and in industry, too. What a performer!

FLUORITE SAMPLES

Fluorite crystal

Blue fluorite crystal

Fluorite

Fluorite

Green fluorite cubic crystal twins

Fluorite jewelry
After quartz, fluorite is the second-most popular mineral for jewelry, because of its enormous range of colors, some of which are very intense.

Fluorite crystal
This mineral is often colorless. However, it can also have a great range of colors—sometimes several in the same crystal. It often cleaves, or splits, into perfect octahedrons.

Group: halides

Formula: CaF_2

Found in: igneous, sedimentary, metamorphic; hydrothermal veins; saline waters in enclosed basins

Main locations: China, Mexico, South Africa, Russia, Spain, Mongolia, Namibia, Kenya, Morocco, Brazil, UK, Italy, Norway, Switzerland, Canada, US

Color: colorless, white, all colors; may be multicolored and banded

Form: octahedral cubes; grains, botryoids, masses, twins

Hardness: 4

Cleavage: parallel to octahedral

Fracture: conchoidal

Luster: vitreous

Streak: white

Specific gravity: 3.0–3.3

Transparency: transparent to translucent

Crystal atlas: cubic

Uses: production of hydrofluoric acid; lenses; plastics; iron and steel industry; added to molten metal to take out impurities; jewelry (as blue john); imitation diamonds; carvings; pottery; ceramic grade for glass and ceramics

Other names: fluor, fluorspar

Lighting up

Fluorite crystals glow brightly, or fluoresce, under ultraviolet (UV) light. The UV light is absorbed and the energy released in the form of visible light, in this case bright blue. Fluorite from two different places may glow two different colors under the same light.

Blue John

This rare banded form of fluorite is only found near Castleton in Derbyshire, England, but has been popular for hundreds of years. Vases found in the ruins of Pompeii, Italy, are rumored to be made from Blue John stone. By the late 18th century, the mineral was in demand for ornamental vases and columns to decorate stately homes. The name comes from the French bleu-jaune, meaning "blue-yellow."

Fluorite lens

Fluorite has been used in lenses in cameras, microscopes, and telescopes. It helps a lens focus, and in telescopes it will work in the far-ultraviolet range, where conventional glasses do not work as well.

Light and dark

In this picture, white cubes of fluorite are embedded in dark, shiny sphalerite crystals (see pages 80–81). Fluorite is a mineral that is found in most of the colors of the rainbow, while sphalerite often contains iron impurities, making it a metallic dark gray or black. Most fluorite is a single color, but some specimens may have multiple colors arranged in bands or zones. When fluorite is free of trace elements, it is transparent and colorless. When sphalerite is black, as it is here, it is called marmatite.

CALCITE

CALCIUM CARBONATE

Calcite crystals

Calcite pseudomorph glendonite

Calcite crystals

Hematite-stained calcite

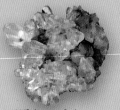

White calcite

When you visit a natural history museum, the building may or may not be made of calcite—but the dinosaur bones inside are. There are more than 300 forms of calcite, and this stuff does everything—from improving soil in farm fields to serving as medicine that helps the body's digestion, from cleaning our homes to lining mine walls to keep dangerous dust from spreading.

Group: carbonates

Formula: $CaCO_3$

Found in: sedimentary, metamorphic; rare in igneous

Main locations: Iceland, Mexico, Germany, Czech Republic, US, England

Color: colorless, white, all colors; may be banded

Form: rhombohedral and scalenohedral crystals, platelike crystals, prisms, flakes, needles; mostly massive but also stalactitic or fibrous

Hardness: 3

Cleavage: rhombohedral, perfect

Fracture: conchoidal (rare, due to perfect cleavage

Luster: vitreous to dull

Streak: white

Specific gravity: 2.7

Transparency: transparent to opaque

Crystal atlas: trigonal

Uses: building materials; cement; aggregate for building roads; optical instruments; purification of iron in blast furnaces; maintaining alkalinity in swimming pools; paper manufacturing; extender in paints; filler in plastics; pharmaceuticals

Other names: calcspar, Iceland spar, dogtooth spar, nailhead spar

Crystalline calcite

This mineral is colorless or white when it is pure, but it can also be found in almost any other color, depending on which trace elements it contains. Calcite is also fluorescent (see page 71).

Dogtooth calcite

These crystals are named for their fanglike shape. They are also called stellar beam calcite: Some claim that they emit beams that connect with extraterrestrials.

CAVE FORMATIONS

In limestone caves across the world, calcite—a major building block of limestone—forms stone icicles and pinnacles. The mineral dissolves in the water that flows through the ground into a cave. The dripping water leaves calcite behind as it travels, and this gradually builds up to form fantastic shapes.

Stalactite

Traces of calcite build up on the ceiling of a cave. Over the years, the stalactite takes shape, hanging down like an icicle. Some calcite drips onto the floor, forming a stalagmite (see below left).

Flowstones

These are perhaps the most common cave formations. They form in thin layers that take on the shapes of the rock underneath. Some look as if they are flowing down the walls of a cave.

Helictites

Some calcite flowstones seem to defy gravity. These helictites grow in any direction, their twisted shapes resulting from many things, ranging from impurities in the calcite to air currents.

Stalagmite

Water dripping from the end of a stalactite leaves calcite on the floor of a cave. The shape builds into a cone and sometimes joins up with the stalactite above it.

Cave pearls

These small, usually rounded stones are formed in a pool of water in a cave and are not attached to the surface of the rock. Layers of calcite slowly gather around a grain of sand or dirt.

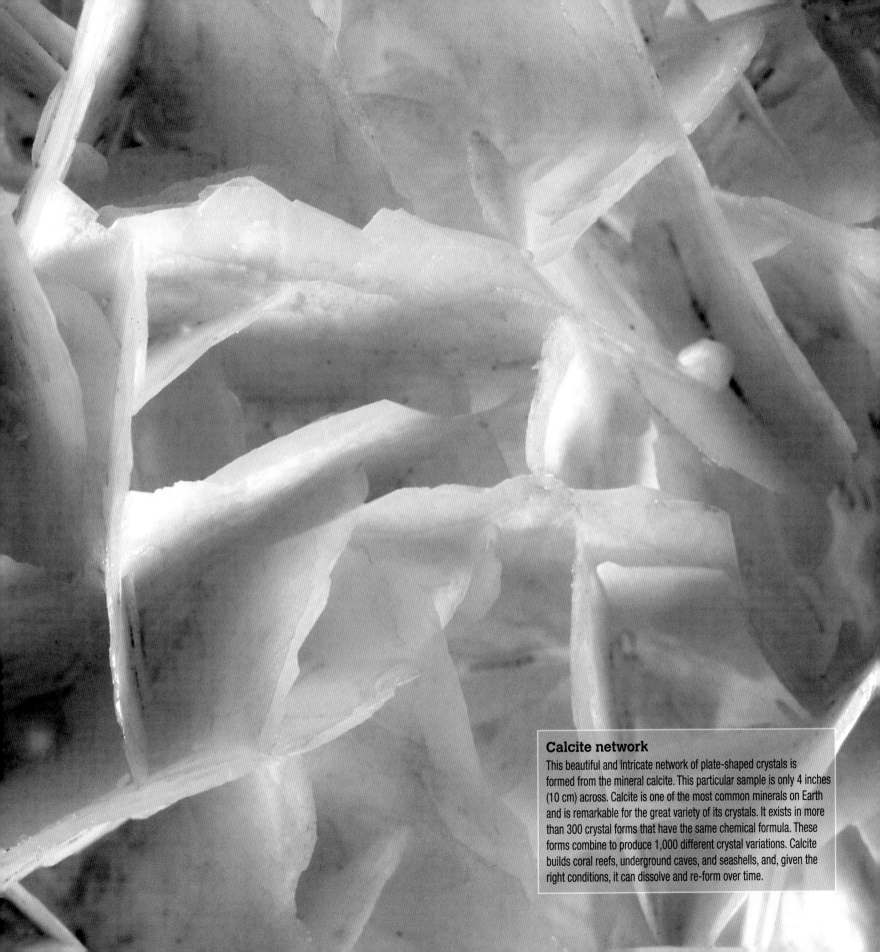

Calcite network

This beautiful and intricate network of plate-shaped crystals is formed from the mineral calcite. This particular sample is only 4 inches (10 cm) across. Calcite is one of the most common minerals on Earth and is remarkable for the great variety of its crystals. It exists in more than 300 crystal forms that have the same chemical formula. These forms combine to produce 1,000 different crystal variations. Calcite builds coral reefs, underground caves, and seashells, and, given the right conditions, it can dissolve and re-form over time.

BARITE

BARIUM SULFATE

Barite is super smooth. It is used in playing cards to add weight and give a silky finish for easy dealing, and in cars to make the bodies smoother. This is no lightweight: It is also used in the oil drilling industry and to block harmful rays in hospitals.

Group: sulfates

Formula: $BaSO_4$

Found in: sedimentary; hydrothermal and mesothermal veins

Main locations: China, India, Morocco, US, Mexico, Turkey, Iran

Color: colorless, white, a wide range of colors; sometimes bluish; may be multicolored and banded

Form: granules, fibres, masses, nodules, stalactites, rosettes; rarely twins; can have cockscomb-like appearance

Hardness: 3–3.5

Cleavage: perfect parallel to base plane, good parallel to prism faces

Fracture: uneven, brittle

Luster: vitreous to pearly

Streak: white

Specific gravity: 4.3–4.6

Transparency: transparent to opaque

Crystal atlas: orthorhombic

Uses: drilling mud (a lubricant used when drilling for oil); paper and rubber manufacturing; plastics; X-rays; rich white pigments; glass manufacturing

Other names: baryte, heavy spar

BARITE SAMPLES

Stalagmitic barite

Hematite-stained barite

Prismatic barite crystal

White barite

Flower of the desert
Some barite in sandy locations forms rosettes that are known as desert roses. Gypsum (see page 129) also forms roses, but they are much thinner, lighter in weight, and more brittle.

Barite crystals
This mineral is the main ore of the metal barium. It is remarkable for its wide range of colors and crystal forms. It is often found around hot springs and in hydrothermal zones. Its name comes from the Greek word *barys*, which means "heavy."

Alchemists' stones
So-called Bologna stones were discovered near Bologna, Italy, in the early 1600s. Made from impure barium, they glow when exposed to light and will glow in the dark for years if heated. Alchemists of the time thought that they possessed magic properties.

Barium meal
A barium "meal" allows doctors to check a patient from the inside. The patient swallows barium liquid, which coats organs so that they can then be examined on an X-ray.

SPHALERITE

ZINC SULFIDE

Sphalerite is named for the Greek word *sphaleros*, which means "treacherous," because it fooled lots of miners into thinking that it was another mineral, such as galena (see pages 54–55), which they wanted for lead. Sphalerite is so weak that it breaks if not cut or polished carefully. However, we rely on it as the most important source of the metal zinc, the coating that keeps metals from rusting.

Rare gemstone
Sphalerite crystals are transparent and strongly colored by varying iron contents. The resulting colors can be fiery and striking. Sphalerite is soft and difficult to cut; it is most often used for pendants and brooches.

Group: sulfides

Formula: (Zn,Fe)S

Found in: sedimentary; hydrothermal zones

Main locations: Australia, Bolivia, Canada, China, India, Ireland, Kazakhstan, Mexico, Peru, US

Color: clear, black, brown, red, orange, yellow; rarely green, gray; may be banded

Form: tetrahedral crystals (usually twinned and grouped), masses, grains, botryoids, stalactites

Hardness: 3.5–4

Cleavage: perfect, parallel to dodecahedron

Fracture: conchoidal

Luster: metallic, submetallic, adamantine, resinous

Streak: white or light brown

Specific gravity: 3.9–4.1

Transparency: transparent to opaque

Crystal atlas: cubic

Uses: jewelry; faceted stones for collectors; as zinc: paints, rubber, cosmetics, plastics, inks, soaps, batteries, textiles, electrical equipment, alloys (such as brass, nickel, silver, and aluminum solder)

Other names: zinc blende, blende, blackjack, steel jack, rosin jack, marmatite

SPHALERITE SAMPLES

Gray sphalerite

Sphalerite and red hematite

Dark gray sphalerite

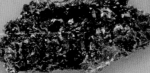

Sphalerite crystals

Sphalerite crystals
This is one of only a few minerals that range so widely in appearance, both in transparency and in color. If it contains a large amount of iron, sphalerite has a dark metallic black color (right). It may fluoresce (see page 71), glowing orange under ultraviolet light.

Galvanized nails

Galvanization is the process of applying a protective zinc coating to another metal, such as iron or steel. The zinc keeps oxygen and water from reaching the metal underneath and so prevents rusting. Even if the coating is scratched, the exposed steel or iron is protected by the remaining zinc.

Metal toys

Many children in the 1950s played with die-cast cars and trucks. These first models of what their parents were driving were possible because they were made with a zinc and aluminum alloy that was easily molded but also lightweight and strong.

Worth less?

The US penny is 97.5 percent zinc and 2.5 percent copper. Zinc has risen so much in price that since 2013, it has cost at least 1.8 cents to mint a single penny!

Food for thought

Humans, animals, and plants all need zinc to grow and develop. It is important for our health because it helps our immune systems function properly. Oysters, beef, and peanuts all contain zinc.

Rare elements

Sphalerite is also the source of various rare elements including iridium (above), cadmium, and gallium. Iridium is a hard, silvery-white transition metal that is more resistant to corrosion than any other metal. It is most frequently alloyed with platinum (see pages 26–27) to harden it.

Chinese lacquer
The art of carving lacquer is unique to China. Often known as cinnabar lacquer, it is colored by powdered mercury sulfide.

Vermilion pigment
From ancient times through to the present day, finely ground cinnabar has been used as a pigment to color paints.

CINNABAR
MERCURY SULFIDE

Named after the ancient Persian for "dragon's blood," deep red cinnabar forms close to volcanic rocks and hot springs—suitably hazardous places for one of the world's most dangerous minerals. When heated, it releases a vapor that can be condensed into liquid mercury, which is highly poisonous. Today it is used only with great care.

Cinnabar mask
This dramatic Peruvian mask, from the 11th century, is made of gold, copper and a red pigment made from cinnabar.

CINNABAR SAMPLES

Cinnabar on dolomite with quartz

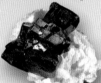

Cinnabar on dolomite

Cinnabar on dolomite

Liquid mercury
Cinnabar is the chief ore of mercury and was extensively mined for the element. Today, because it is so dangerous, mercury is being replaced with nontoxic substitutes.

Group:	sulfides
Formula:	HgS
Found in:	igneous; hydrothermal zones; hot springs; often associated with volcanic activity
Main locations:	Spain, China, Italy, Slovenia, Serbia, US, Russia, Outer Mongolia
Color:	all shades of red, from bright to dark
Form:	masses, encrustations, granules, globes, thick tabular crystals
Hardness:	2–2.5
Cleavage:	perfect prismatic
Fracture:	uneven
Luster:	adamantine, submetallic, dull
Streak:	red
Specific gravity:	8.0–8.1
Transparency:	transparent to opaque
Crystal atlas:	trigonal
Uses:	Chinese traditional medicines; artists' paints; mercury production; enamels
Other names:	cinnabarite, vermilion

Cinnabar moth
The cinnabar moth flies by both day and night and can be found across Europe and Asia. It is named for its bright red markings.

ARSENOPYRITE

IRON ARSENIC SULFIDE

This mineral often forms alongside silver, gold, and tin, and miners have to get rid of it to reach their targets. It also smells of garlic if you hit it with a hammer! But that scent is a clue to an unwelcome fact—it is a source of the deadly poison arsenic. However, arsenic has a useful side. It has medical applications, and is used in paints and dyes for clothing, and for bricks that line furnaces.

ARSENOPYRITE SAMPLES

Arsenopyrite (silver-gray) and fluorite (purple)

Silver-gray arsenopyrite

Realgar (arsenic sulfide)

Orpiment (arsenic sulfide)

Group: sulfides

Formula: FeAsS

Found in: igneous, sedimentary, metamorphic; hydrothermal zones

Main locations: China, Bolivia, Mexico, Portugal, Germany, Norway, Sweden, US, Canada, Japan

Color: silver-white to steel gray; tarnishes to a pale copper color on exposure to air

Form: elongated crystals, columns, grains, masses, compact aggregates; sometimes twins

Hardness: 5.5–6.5

Cleavage: good, parallel to dome faces

Fracture: uneven

Luster: metallic

Streak: grayish black

Specific gravity: 5.9–6.2

Transparency: opaque

Crystal atlas: monoclinic

Uses: the principal ore of arsenic; dyes; chemicals; leather treatment; insecticides; pigments; wood preservatives

Other names: arsenical pyrites, mispickel

Arsenopyrite
The well-formed crystals of arsenopyrite have sharp acute angles. The mineral may contain a small amount of gold as an impurity, and it is sometimes mistaken for fool's gold, or pyrite (see pages 30–31).

Geothermal pools
The Champagne Pool, in the Waiotapu area of New Zealand, has colorful waters with a temperature of 165°F (75°C). The colors are due to arsenic, antimony, and mercury sulfides.

ARSENIC

Arsenic has a murderous history and is known by many as the king of poisons. From Roman times to the mid-nineteenth century, it reigned supreme because its lack of color, smell, and taste made it difficult to detect. It was not always used with the intention to kill. Some took it for strength and others to enhance their beauty. Few realized how dangerous it was.

Cesare Borgia
The Borgias were a famous ruling family in Italy during the Renaissance. They were accused of poisoning many people with arsenic in order to gain control of their money.

Arsenic eaters
In 1851, a Swiss physician published an article about the practice of arsenic eating in Styria (now Austria). Peasants in the region were eating arsenic regularly to help their breathing when they were walking or working high in the mountains. No study was done, but it is likely that they were slowly poisoning themselves.

Beauty treatments
This poster from 1910 advertizes a hotel in the Italian Alps that boasts thermal baths rich in mineral salts that include arsenic. In the same decade, Dr. Campbell's arsenic wafers claimed to "remove Pimples, Wrinkles, Freckles, Black Heads, Vulgar Redness and all beauty-marring defects." Fortunately, the use of this stopped in the 1930s.

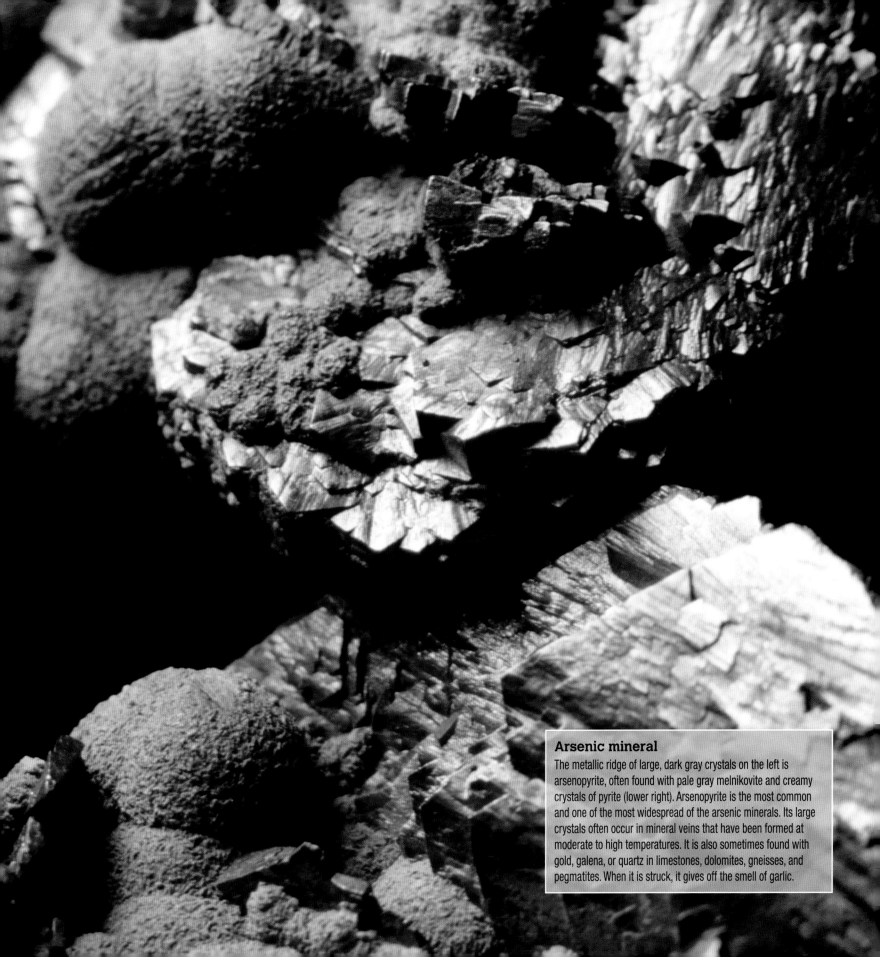

Arsenic mineral

The metallic ridge of large, dark gray crystals on the left is arsenopyrite, often found with pale gray melnikovite and creamy crystals of pyrite (lower right). Arsenopyrite is the most common and one of the most widespread of the arsenic minerals. Its large crystals often occur in mineral veins that have been formed at moderate to high temperatures. It is also sometimes found with gold, galena, or quartz in limestones, dolomites, gneisses, and pegmatites. When it is struck, it gives off the smell of garlic.

Rocks are solids made of minerals. They form Earth's crust. We stand on rocks, build with them, turn them into statues, use them as tools, wear them—we can even eat one kind of rock! If all the living organisms, water, and soil were taken off our planet, all that would be left behind would be rock.

ROCKS

IGNEOUS ROCK GALLERY

Igneous rock once flowed deep underground as thick, sticky magma. This hot, molten "soup" is made of a mix of elements and compounds, each with their own characteristics, such as the temperature at which they freeze to a solid. This is how different types of igneous rock are made.

Graphic granite

Olivine gabbro

Diabase with plagioclase phenocrysts

Porphyritic granite

Pumice

Dolerite

Basalt

Amygdaloidal basalt

Scoria

Luxulyanite hydrothermal granite

Ash containing lava (xenolith)

Tourmaline and quartz in granite

Tuff

Gneiss

Diabase with plagioclase phenocrysts

Mica-rich granite

Bedded tuff

Gabbro

Icelandic lava
This single piece of rock shows two types of lava flow—aa and pahoehoe flows (see page 94). The aa, top right, is a jumbled pile of loose, rough rock, while the pahoehoe has a smooth, ropey appearance.

Snowflake obsidian

Porphyritic granite

Diorite

GRANITE

INTRUSIVE IGNEOUS ROCK

Power, glory, the strongest of beliefs—leaders of nations have turned their aspirations and ideas into monuments that will stand for all time. And they have built these monuments from granite. The Pyramids of Giza, the Great Wall of China, and the base of the Statue of Liberty were all hewn from granite, the most durable of all rocks.

GRANITE SAMPLES

Graphic striated granite

Tourmaline and quartz in granite

Porphyritic granite

Luxullianite hydrothermal granite

Rock type: igneous, felsic, plutonic

Main locations: worldwide, most commonly in batholiths

Major minerals: amphibole, biotite, feldspar, hornblende, biotite muscovite, plagioclase, pyroxene, quartz

Color: white, black, and gray to pink, orange, and red

Form: intrusive, with a pitted surface

Texture: fine to coarse grained

Weather impact: resistant

Uses: building material; pavements and curbstones; statues; gravestones; jewelry; curling stones; marbles

Granite landscape

Over 50 million years, glaciers and rivers have carved out the granite landscape of Yosemite Valley in eastern California. Today, impressive granite formations tower over the valley. The highest peak is Mount Lyell, at 13,114 feet (4,000 m).

Walking on granite

The most common rock in Earth's continental crust, granite cools from silica-rich magma deep underground. It forms great lumps of rock, or batholiths, that can stretch for hundreds of miles.

ROCK OF ANCIENT EGYPT

To the ancient Egyptians, death was the beginning of a magnificent journey. Pharaohs were buried inside great granite tombs and celebrated with immense granite statues. To carve the granite, workers used quartz sand, which acted as a sandpaper, with their saws and drills.

Pharaoh sphinx
This red granite sphinx depicts one of the very few female Egyptian pharaohs, Hatshepsut, complete with royal beard.

Granite god
This granite statue shows the falcon-headed god Horus protecting a pharaoh. The falcon's right eye was the Sun, or morning star, representing power, and its left eye was the Moon, or evening star, representing healing.

Ancient words
Ancient Egyptians carved hieroglyphs ("sacred carvings") in solid granite using wooden mallets and copper chisels.

Carved stone
This granite head of Sesostris III, pharaoh from 1836 to 1818 BCE, is from the Temple of Amun.

Building blocks
Workers hauled granite more than 500 miles (800 km), from Aswan in southern Egypt to Giza in the north, for the pyramid of the pharaoh Khufu. Granite beams weighing up to 66 tons were used for the King's Chamber, deep inside.

BASALT

EXTRUSIVE IGNEOUS ROCK

Basalt has it covered. It is the most common rock on Earth, forming much of the bedrock of the planet's crust under the oceans. It is on the Moon, Mercury, Mars, and Venus, too. When blasted out of volcanoes it is so fluid that it can flow for hundreds of miles. Gas bubbles can make it coarse, and it is tough enough to be used for roads and pavements.

Rock type: igneous, volcanic, mafic

Main locations: worldwide where volcanoes have erupted; ocean floor

Major minerals: plagioclase feldspars, pyroxene, olivine; sometimes quartz, leucite, nepheline

Color: dark gray, black; sometimes with a greenish or reddish crust

Form: masses, rough, grainy (aa); ropy (pahoehoe); vesicular (with holes caused by volcanic gases); pillowy

Texture: fine grained

Weather impact: resistant

Uses: foundations, cobblestones, statues, floor tiles

BASALT SAMPLES

Amygdaloidal basalt

Vesicular basalt

Fossil leaves in ash from Vesuvius

Vesuvius lava bomb

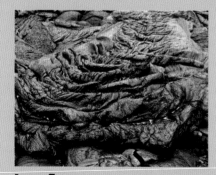

Lava flows
When mafic lava cools quickly it turns to basalt. A pahoehoe lava flow like this one has a smooth glassy surface that wrinkles as it cools, becoming solid rock while lava continues to flow beneath it.

Corded lava
When lava solidifies with a smooth, ropy surface it is called pahoehoe, or corded lava, because it looks like loops of rope. This piece of lava is from the area around Mount Vesuvius, near Naples, Italy.

Buddhist statues
These Buddhist carvings are in the Ellora Caves in central India, near Aurangabad. These 34 monasteries and temples were carved out of a tall basalt cliff between 200 BCE and 1000 CE and extend for more than a mile (2 km). They are in the Maharasthra volanic formation in an area that contains nearly 1,200 such caves.

Basalt is the most common rock in Earth's crust—70 percent of Earth's surface, including all the oceans, rests on basalt.

Aztec calendar
The Stone of the Sun, the Aztec calendar stone, weighs 25 tons and is carved in porphyritic basalt. It was carved in the 16th century and divides the year into 18 months of 20 days each.

Giant's Causeway
One of the most famous examples of columnar basalt is the Giant's Causeway in Antrim, Northern Ireland. These polygonal columns were the result of a volcanic eruption 60 million years ago. Legend has it that they were carved from the coast by a giant, Finn McCool.

Olympus Mons
Basalt does not exist only on Earth. It covers the surface of Mercury, Venus, Mars, and the Moon. The most spectacular geological feature and the highest mountain on Mars, Olympus Mons, is the largest known volcano in our solar system. Its central caldera and gentle slopes have been formed from basalt lava flows.

PEGMATITE

INTRUSIVE IGNEOUS ROCK

PEGMATITE SAMPLES

Granite pegmatite

Pegmatite, columbite, quartz, and apatite

Pink pegmatite and muscovite

Gilbertite, pegmatite, and vayrynenite

Pegmatite, petalite, and pyrophyllite

This rock is a treasure chest—hard to find, and possibly full of the rarest gems. Pegmatite forms deep underground, where magma cools slowly and produces large crystals. Hidden inside the rock are some of the most sought-after minerals, including topaz and aquamarine, spodumene and beryl.

Rock type: igneous, felsic, plutonic

Main locations: in high, rugged terrains; most commonly occurring in batholiths

Major minerals: apatite, beryl, feldspar, fluorite, garnet, lepidolite, quartz, muscovite, spodumene, topaz, tourmaline, emerald, aquamarine, cassiterite

Color: black, brown, cream, green-gray, pink, red, rust, silver, white, yellow

Form: intrusive, with interlocking crystals

Texture: medium to very coarse grained

Weather impact: resistant

Uses: architecture and building facings; countertops and tiles; electronic devices (as mica); glass, ceramics, fillers (as feldspar); jewelry; sculptures

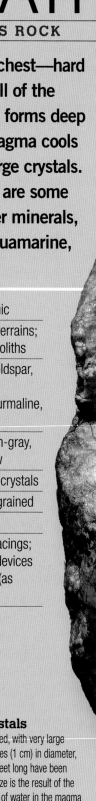

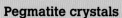

Pegmatite crystals
This rock is coarse grained, with very large crystals at least 0.4 inches (1 cm) in diameter, although crystals many feet long have been reported. The crystals' size is the result of the cooling rate and amount of water in the magma that allows cooling to be very gradual.

Writing tip
Among the rare minerals that are found in pegmatites are those that contain tungsten. This hard, steel-gray metal has the highest melting point of all the metals. As tungsten carbide, it is extremely hard and is used for cutting tools and armor-piercing ammunition as well as the tips of ballpoint pens.

Painted walls
The Painted Wall on the north side of Black Canyon of the Gunnison National Park is the tallest sheer cliff in Colorado, at 2,250 feet (690 m). Large areas of intrusive igneous rock like this are called batholiths. Lighter-colored bands, or dikes, of younger pegmatite rock slice through the canyon's granite walls.

Pegmatite seam
Pegmatite is the result of water-rich magma, so it is the last rock to cool and harden. Because it remains fluid longer, it is able to squeeze into cracks in rocks. This is how it formed bright pink stripes on the Painted Wall of the Black Canyon.

Mineral rich
Pegmatites are sometimes the source of spodumene (above), a valuable mineral that is an ore of the silver-white metal lithium, used in everyday objects such as medicines and batteries.

A beryl crystal **27 feet (8 m) long** and **4.5 feet (1.4 m) wide** was found in pegmatite in **Maine.**

Golden topaz
Gem-quality topaz deposits are found in pegmatites, sometimes producing huge, flawless crystals. Cut stones in many different colors are used for all kinds of jewelry, including this gold and pink topaz necklace.

Tourmaline earrings
Spectacular crystals of the gem tourmaline (see pages 170–171) have been found in pegmatite. This gem is found in more colors than any other mineral is.

Treasure trove
Beryl-rich pegmatites are incredibly rare. Scientists estimate that beryls such as this blue aquamarine are found in only 0.003 percent of Earth's entire body of magma.

Volcanic wilderness

The volcanoes of the 750-mile-long (1,200 km) Kamchatka Peninsula, in Russia, are among the most active in the world. Some 33 of the 300 total volcanoes are currently erupting, and most are explosive. Since 1690, 200 eruptions have been recorded. The dynamic beauty of the area is fraught with danger—not just from the volcanoes but also from lava streams, cinder fields, geysers, and hot springs. Most of the volcanoes are made of basalt, which usually forms shield volcanoes, or of andesite, which forms cone volcanoes.

TUFF

EXTRUSIVE IGNEOUS ROCK

Tuff starts with a bang—the big bang that takes place when a volcano erupts and blasts out rock, ash, and magma. Whatever lands and forms a rock is called tuff. There are three kinds of tuff: crystal, vitric (made mainly of glass), and lithic (made up of chunks of broken rock).

Rock type: igneous, felsic, pyroclastic

Main locations: near all the largest volcanoes worldwide

Major minerals: in felsic or rhyolitic tuff, feldspar or quartz; in basaltic or mafic tuff, feldspar, pyroxene, or olivine

Color: brown, gray, yellow; whitish gray or gray powder when newly fallen

Form: welded and compacted matter from volcanic eruptions; a mixture of rock fragments, crystals, and glass shards; pumice is common

Texture: fine grained

Weather impact: not resistant

Uses: construction stone cladding; walls; flooring; paving stones; sculptures

TUFF SAMPLES

Uncompacted ignimbrite

Welded ignimbrite

Bedded tuff

Tuff block

Welded ignimbrite

Tuff villages
Over centuries, the tuff in southwestern Tuscany, Italy, has been carved to form houses, cellars, and tombs. Medieval villages such as Pitigliano rise majestically out of the stone hillsides.

Tuff and lava

Tuff is a soft, porous rock formed from compacted volcanic ash and dust. This tuff envelops a xenolith, a fragment of darker-colored lava. Some tuff deposits are hundreds of feet thick because of successive eruptions from a particular volcano.

VESUVIUS, 79 CE

It was noon on August 24, and the people of Pompeii and Herculaneum, in southern Italy, were going about their daily business. Suddenly, Mount Vesuvius exploded, sending a 10-mile (16 km) cloud of ash and a hail of pumice (see pages 102–103) into the sky. Just 24 hours later, more than 2,500 citizens of the two cities were dead, suffocated by lethal clouds of toxic gas and buried under a devastating flood of volcanic mud and rock.

Vesuvius erupting

The eruption lasted for two days. Giant surge clouds, or pyroclastic flows, of hot ash steamed down the mountain's sides, burning and suffocating the two cities.

Uncovering Pompeii

Beginning in the 1850s, people dug for treasure in Pompeii. Things changed when Giuseppe Fiorelli took over in 1860 (left). He began to excavate from the top down, thus preserving many of the buildings.

Pompeii today

Mount Vesuvius is the only active volcano on the mainland of Europe. The last major eruption was in 1631, and the last minor one in 1944. The 700,000 people who live around the mountain's flanks may well find themselves in danger in the future.

Pompeii dog

Archaeologists have found cavities in the ash, left by the bodies of those who died. By filling the cavities with plaster, they have captured the exact moments of death of both humans and animals.

Easter Island

Perhaps the most famous statues in the world, the *moai* of Easter Island in the South Pacific, are carved mostly out of tuff. Tuff erodes easily, so few of the original designs have survived.

PUMICE

EXTRUSIVE IGNEOUS ROCK

When is rock like a fizzy drink? When it is pumice! Sometimes, when volcanoes erupt, gases dissolve in the magma and form tiny bubbles, making the lava froth like a shaken can of soda. When the rock hardens, it is full of holes that make it so light that it floats.

Rock type: igneous, felsic, pyroclastic

Main locations: near volcanoes worldwide (but may be carried thousands of miles away by the wind)

Major minerals: mainly volcanic glass, iron oxides, silica, with rare minerals: in felsic or rhyolitic tuff, feldspar or quartz; in basaltic or mafic tuff, feldspar, olivine or pyroxene

Color: colorless, beige, light gray, light green, pink, white, yellow-gray

Form: welded and compacted matter from eruptions; may or may not contain crystals

Texture: fine grained

Weather impact: not resistant

Uses: snow traction control mixes for roads; Lava soap; dental polishes and toothpastes; industrial polishes; decorative ground covers in planters; conditioner for stone-washed denim; traction enhancer in tire rubber; cat litter

Pumice stone field
The Campo de Piedra Pomez in Argentina has more than 5,000 superb rock formations in an area that is only 16 by 6 miles (25 by 10 km). The dry, harsh winds have sculpted the pumice rocks into a white labyrinth.

PUMICE SAMPLES

Stratified (layered) pumice

Highly porous pumice

Fibrous pumice

Ejected block of fibrous pumice

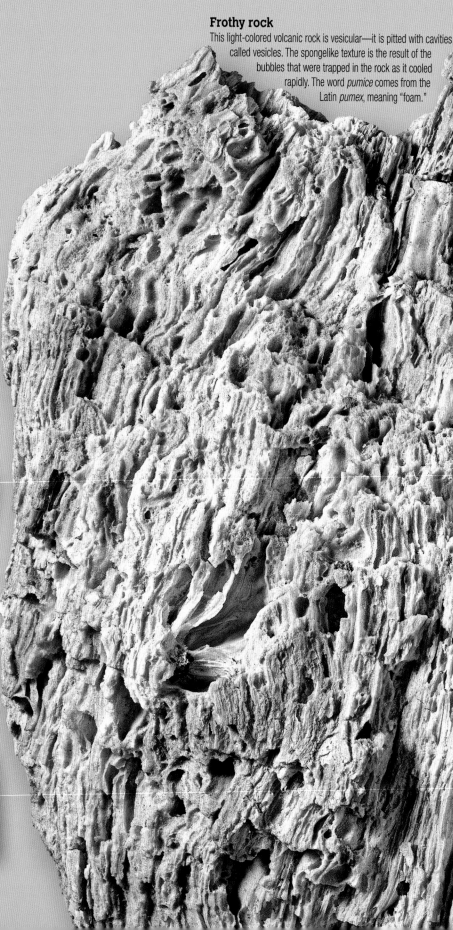

Frothy rock
This light-colored volcanic rock is vesicular—it is pitted with cavities called vesicles. The spongelike texture is the result of the bubbles that were trapped in the rock as it cooled rapidly. The word *pumice* comes from the Latin *pumex*, meaning "foam."

In the 1991 **Mount Pinatubo** eruption in the **Philippines**, more than 1.2 cubic miles (5 cu km) of **ash** and **pumice lapilli** were blasted out.

pumice raft —

new island —

Floating raft
In August 2006, NASA's Aqua satellite spotted two exciting new features about the Tonga Islands in the South Pacific. One was a new island, emerging because of an underwater eruption. The second was the enormous raft of pumice that resulted.

Scoria
This basaltic lava is also vesicular, but its bubble cavities are much smaller than pumice's, so the rock is much heavier. It does not float. This particular piece is from Vesuvius (see page 101).

Foot scrub
Pumice is excellent for exfoliating—rubbing away dead skin—and is used as a body scrub.

Lightweight dome
The Pantheon in Rome was built by the emperor Hadrian from 118 to 125 CE, as a temple dedicated to the gods. Its magnificent domed roof is supported by intersecting arches balanced on eight piers. The Romans used the lightest material of all for the dome—pumice.

OBSIDIAN

EXTRUSIVE IGNEOUS ROCK

Break a piece of obsidian, and the pieces are sharp enough to cut—so Stone Age people used it as a blade. Obsidian is a comparatively young rock. It forms when lava cools and becomes solid glass so fast that crystals have no time to grow, so it has a smooth, glassy look. However, after 20 million years of slowly absorbing moisture, it will go cloudy.

Rock type: igneous, felsic

Main locations: near volcanoes worldwide where lava is cooled very rapidly

Major minerals: almost total absence, but may contain alkali feldspar and quartz

Color: black, blue, brown, green, orange, tan, yellow

Form: volcanic glass produced from felsic lava with minimum crystal growth

Texture: glassy; may have phenocrysts

Weather impact: resistant

Uses: ornaments; carvings; jewelry; medical instruments

Cutting edge
Obsidian is very hard and brittle, and it fractures to give very sharp edges. In the Aztec kingdom (13th–15th centuries), obsidian knives (above) were used for both sacrifices and medical purposes.

OBSIDIAN SAMPLES

Spherulitic (with radiating crystals) obsidian

Snowflake obsidian

Obsidian with conchoidal fractures

Pitchstone

Obsidian cliff
In Yellowstone Park, in Wyoming, a vertical cliff towers above Obsidian Creek. Obsidian was first quarried from this cliff to make tools more than 11,000 years ago. The cliff was used as a source through the following centuries, and the obsidian was traded as far north as Canada.

Snowflake dog
In some obsidian rocks, small white crystals of cristobalite cluster together in the glass to produce a distinctive snowflake pattern (left). When polished, some obsidian also displays different colors and is known as fireworks obsidian.

Jeweled glass
From the earliest times, the natural brilliance of obsidian has had an appeal. Obsidian jewelry dating back thousands of years has been found at many ancient archaeological sites. Jewelers today are no less interested in this ancient stone.

Apache tear
It is said that a party of Apache warriors was once ambushed by an enemy tribe. Rather than be captured, they rode their horses over a cliff to their deaths. The tears of their families froze when they hit the ground to become the "Apache tears" we know today.

Obsidian mask
In the Aztec kingdom, masks were often used as ornaments, although they were also sometimes worn during rituals. This miniature mask is believed to represent Ixtlilton, the lieutenant of the god of war, Huitzilopochtli.

Glassy rock
Obsidian is a natural glass with a smooth texture that is produced when hot, silica-rich lava spews out of a volcano. Pure obsidian is usually dark, but the color varies depending on impurities. Different volcanoes produce different types of obsidian.

Obsidian band

In central Oregon lies Newberry National Volcanic Monument, more than 54,000 acres (22,000 ha) of some of the most spectacular geological scenery created by volcanic activity. In addition to beautiful lakes, there are many volcanic features, including cinder cones, lava caves, basalt flows, and rhyolite flows of obsidian. This particular large rock formation has been cracked by weather and erosion, but the band of black obsidian is easy to see. The volcano is still active, most recently erupting only about 1,300 years ago.

GABBRO

INTRUSIVE IGNEOUS ROCK

Gabbro is tough. It sits under the basalt of Earth's crust in vast amounts, the most abundant rock in that layer of the planet. When gabbro is exposed, it weathers to form jagged mountain peaks. It is sometimes called black granite—but it is not like that rock, being darker, denser, and heavier.

Rock type: igneous, mafic, plutonic

Main locations: oceanic crust

Major minerals: mainly plagioclase feldspar, such as labradorite or bytownite, and pyroxene; also augite, olivine

Color: dark gray to black, speckled with white; may have black, brown, or red spots

Form: created when molten magma is trapped, instead of reaching the surface to cool as basalt

Texture: coarse grained

Weather impact: resistant

Uses: ornamental paving and building facings; kitchen surfaces; crushed stone and aggregates

Looking closer
This colored micrograph of a thin section of gabbro shows how the minerals in the rock—olivine and plagioclase feldspar—knit together. Olivine has numerous irregularly shaped and randomly oriented crystals. Plagioclase felspar forms long, slender crystals.

Troctolite

Weathered olivine gabbro

olivine gabbro

Crusty rock
The deeper rocks of Earth's oceanic crust are usually gabbro. The rock has large crystals, so it looks speckled. It resembles basalt, but it is more coarsely grained.

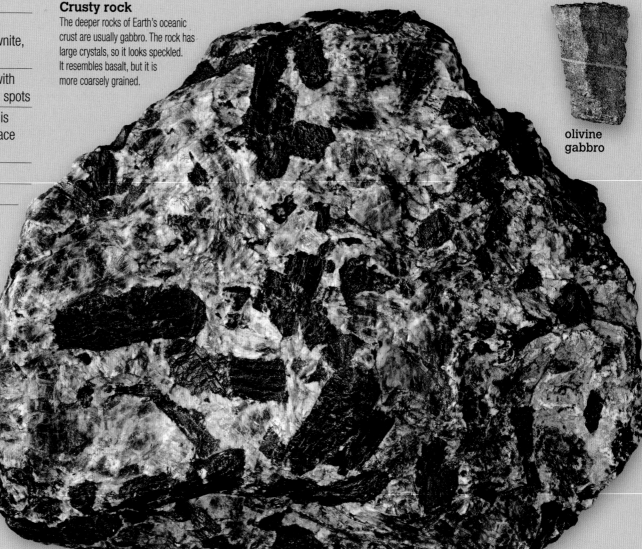

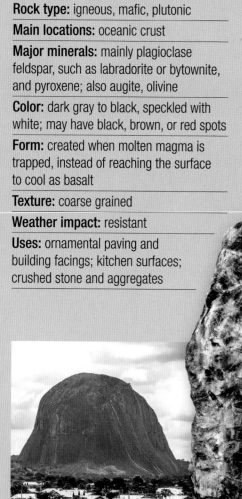

Zuma Rock, Nigeria
At 2,380 feet (725 m), Zuma Rock is hard to miss! It is even depicted on the country's currency, on the 100-naira note. This magnificent gabbro and granodiorite rock is close to Nigeria's capital, Abuja.

DOLERITE

INTRUSIVE IGNEOUS ROCK

Uncertainty about the identity of dolerite is evident from its many names, including diabase, whin, whinstone, trap, and traprock. It is extremely hard; like gabbro, it is dark in color and has a speckled appearance because its crystals are usually large enough to be visible to the naked eye.

Rock type: igneous, mafic, aphanitic

Main locations: dikes, sills, lopoliths, and laccoliths near volcanoes worldwide

Major minerals: mainly plagioclase feldspar and pyroxene; also quartz, chlorite, orthoclase, magnetite

Color: dark gray to black; may be mottled black and white

Form: a kind of basalt that contains relatively little silica

Texture: fine to medium grained

Weather impact: resistant

Uses: roads; railway ballast; monuments; inlays; jewelry

DOLERITE SAMPLES

Fine-grained quartz enstatite dolerite

Dolerite slab

Weathered dolerite

Weathered honeycomb dolerite

Death Valley rock
Mushroom Rock in Death Valley, CA, has been carved from hard dolerite by sand and weather. It is an example of a hoodoo, a pillar of rock left by erosion.

Speckled stone
Dolerite ranges in color from gray to black and is often mottled in appearance. Many of the older dolerites were formed during the breakup of Earth's crustal plates.

The **2,460-foot-thick (750 m) Golden Mile Dolerite** in Kalgoorlie, **Australia**, is **host** to one of the most famous **gold deposits** in the world.

Dolerite circle
About 3,000 years ago, some Stone Age people carted heavy dolerite stones some 150 miles (240 km) from Wales to England to form part of a massive stone circle. No one is sure why or how they did this, but Stonehenge still stands today for all to see.

SEDIMENTARY ROCKS

Sedimentary rock forms in layers. Sediment, mud, or sand at the bottom of a lake or sea is compacted or cemented until it forms a solid. This happens time and again to create many different layers. Each layer is like a page in a book telling us about Earth in the past.

Burgess shale, with primitive arthropod fossil

Clastic sedimentary conglomerate

Limestone with marine shells

Conglomerate with granite schists

Rock gypsum

Flint

Halite (rock salt)

Halite (rock salt)

Green copper-stained sandstone

Gypsum

Sandstone

Sandstone containing micas

Polished
red jasper

Sandstone
with impact
striations

Lignite

Flint

Tuff

Pebbly breccia
conglomerate

Breccia

Bituminous
coal

Desert rose
These "flowers" are
usually formed from
gypsum or barite, although
some are celestine or other
minerals. They form in very
dry conditions, usually deserts,
and are created in only tens
to hundreds of years —a very
short time, in geological terms.

Marl

LIMESTONE
SEDIMENTARY CARBONATE

Limestone is alive! Well, sort of. It is made partly of the shells and bones of long-dead creatures, so a limestone building in the middle of the city might contain bits of dinosaur bone! This is the third-most abundant sedimentary rock (after mudstone and sandstone), so it features in many landscapes.

Rock type: sedimentary, marine

Main locations: continental crust, from rocks formed in warm, shallow seas

Major minerals: mainly calcite and aragonite; also dolomite, quartz

Color: most commonly white, yellow, brown, gray to black; darker when rich in oil

Form: usually in masses, can be banded; may contain fragments of intact reef structures

Texture: fine to very coarse grained

Weather impact: variable

Uses: construction; facings; floor tiles; weather- and heat-resistant roofing; soil treatment for agriculture; safety dust to seal mine walls; iron production; glass-making; cement manufacture

LIMESTONE SAMPLES

Red limestone with gastropods

Oolitic limestone

Algal boundstone

Lithographic limestone

Nummulitic limestone

Rocky landscape
Limestone pavements sometimes form. These are composed of slabs of rock called clint, which are separated by large vertical cracks called grikes. They are formed after limestone is dissolved by rainwater that contains carbon dioxide.

Dragonfly fossil
Sometimes creatures without hard shells can be fossilized after falling into lime muds. The muds lithify (transform into stone) around the insect remains, leaving some dark organic matter.

Shergotty Meteorite

Limestone is mainly calcium carbonate, which exists only on Earth—and perhaps on Mars. On August 25, 1865, an 11-pound (5 kg) meteorite fell to Earth in India. It is believed to have broken off from the crust of Mars, and it contains a little calcium carbonate and traces of gypsum (see page 129).

Soft rock

Limestone is a soft rock in that calcite is a softer material than many of the silicates found in other rocks. However, when well-cemented it can be pretty tough. It is usually made up of tiny fossils of marine organisms, shell fragments, and other fossil debris. These fossils can often be seen with the naked eye.

BUILDING WITH LIMESTONE

Limestone is so tough that it has been used to construct buildings for thousands of years, either as rock or crushed to powder. Those ancient master builders, the Romans, made the most durable concrete by mixing volcanic ash with lime extracted from limestone that they baked at 1,650°F (900°C). Today, limestone is still a valuable resource.

Mayan pyramid

The pyramid of El Castillo is at the center of Chichén Itzá, the ancient city of the Maya established in 100 CE, in today's Mexico. The city sits on a limestone plateau, and the rock was used for its buildings.

Leaning tower

In 1173, workers began a new bell tower for the cathedral of Pisa in Italy. Built of limestone with a marble facing, it proved too heavy for the clay soil and began to lean when they reached the third floor.

Tower of London

The main building of this notorious prison, the White Tower, was built in 1078 by William the Conqueror. Its builders used English limestone, but the facing is limestone quarried and shipped in from Caen, France.

Empire State Building

Limestone from Indiana was used to build one of the most famous buildings in the world, the Empire State Building. The quarry supplied 18,630 tons of stone.

The White House

The pure white limestone that was used in the 1902 renovation of the White House may have come from quarries on the island of Brac, in the Adriatic Sea. However, all records were destroyed in World War II.

Time capsules

Limestone stalagmites lean crazily at all angles in an amazing cave in Borneo. Earthquake activity has meant that the cave is now known as the Drunken Forest Cave. Borneo has some of the largest cave systems in the world. In 2012, researchers took samples from more than 1,700 stalagmites in three separate caves in northern Borneo. By analyzing the minerals in these time capsules, they have provided a better understanding of how the western Pacific responded to any abrupt climate changes over a period of tens of thousands of years.

CHALK

CALCIUM CARBONATE

Chalk cliffs that tower over the waters of southern England were built up under the sea about 100 million years ago. Chalk is white because it formed in warm, shallow seas from the shells of tiny marine animals and calcite oozes, away from the land and away from any contamination by sand, mud, or other sediment.

Rock type: sedimentary, marine, form of limestone

Main locations: worldwide in rocks of the Cretaceous period (140–65 mya)

Major minerals: mainly calcite; some silica or clay minerals

Color: white, yellow, gray

Form: soft, powdery rock; can contain fossil shells

Texture: fine grained

Weather impact: not resistant

Uses: cement for building; fertilizer for farmland; iron and steel manufacture; filling powder in pastes and foods

CHALK SAMPLES

Red chalk

Marcasite in chalk

Stylolitic chalk

Contorted (slump-folded) chalk

Clean rock
Chalk is a soft, fine-textured type of limestone that is easy to spot because it is so white. It is porous—full of tiny holes through which liquid or air can pass quickly. This means that chalk landscapes are often rather dry and bare.

Coastal erosion
Over time, acids in seawater dissolve some types of coastal rock. The chalk of steep cliffs like these in southern England is shaped over centuries by the combination of weathering and seawater erosion.

Land of caves
In the rolling hills of Bet Guvrin-Maresha National Park in Israel are underground caverns carved from the soft chalk. For more than 2,000 years, 3,500 chambers have been used as burial sites, dovecotes, storerooms, and hiding places.

Drawing with chalk
Chalk helped create the first cave drawings, and in the Renaissance it was made into sticks for artists. Although traditionally composed of natural chalk, modern blackboard chalk is usually made from the mineral gypsum.

Coccoliths
Chalk is made up of tiny calcium carbonate plates called coccoliths. These plates are formed by single-celled algae called coccolithophores. Some coccolithophore fossils date back 500 million years.

Anti-slip
How can ancient plankton help modern athletes? The shells of these tiny creatures formed the chalk that is crushed to powder and used to reduce friction. Gymnasts rub it on their hands when using the uneven bars.

The white **chalk cliffs** of **Étretat** in northern France, famous for their **natural arches**, inspired paintings by the artist **Claude Monet**.

BRECCIA

SEDIMENTARY CLASTIC ROCK

A landslide or avalanche often sees the birth of breccia. Broken fragments of pebbles and older rocks become stuck together by fine, sandy material to form new rock. This happens so quickly that the hard edges of the rock are not rubbed into curves by movement, so there are sharp edges.

Rock type: sedimentary, marine, freshwater, glacial

Main locations: often at fault zones or unconformities; may be near conglomerates

Major minerals: calcite, feldspar, quartz, silica

Color: many colors, from black through orange and purple to yellow and white

Form: angular, broken fragments of minerals or rock, cemented together

Texture: coarse grained (mixture of fine to medium grains and angular fragments of pebble to boulder size)

Weather impact: resistant

Uses: architectural stone; windowsills; tiles; aggregate for road construction

Conglomerates
These sedimentary rocks are like breccia but have been formed by large, rounded, well-weathered pebbles, stones, or boulders that are cemented together.

Sinkhole in the Bahamas
Breccia forms when violent action breaks up rock and it reforms quickly. This can happen during a landslide, at a fault zone, in a collapsed cave, or when a sinkhole suddenly appears.

BRECCIA SAMPLES

Tillite, a breccia conglomerate

Carbonatitic volcanic breccia

Pebbly conglomerate

Breccia
Breccia has large, angular fragments, or clasts, that are cemented together by smaller particles. The word *breccia* is actually Latin for "broken."

SHALE

SEDIMENTARY CLASTIC ROCK

Much of Earth's surface is covered by shale, the most common sedimentary rock. The rock forms in thin layers, so it flakes easily. Black shale can be a source of oil and gas because it contains organic material from decomposed plankton, bacteria, and plant matter.

Rock type: sedimentary, marine, freshwater

Main locations: rocks from deep-sea deposits where slow-moving waters deposited fine sediments

Major minerals: mainly clay minerals; minor amounts of quartz, silica, albite, biotite, calcite, chlorite, dolomite, hematite, mica, pyrite

Color: black, brown, green, gray, red, yellow, blue

Form: finely bedded layers in a wide range of thicknesses

Texture: very fine grained

Weather impact: not very resistant

Uses: tiles; bricks; source of oil and natural gas; cement; pottery; furnace linings

Crushed shale
When some shales are crushed and mixed with water, they produce clays that can be made into useful pots. Crushed shale can also be used to make clay tennis courts.

Layered
Shale is fine-grained rock made of mud that contains a mixture of silt and at least 30 percent clay minerals. It is a layered rock that splits easily into thin slices. The higher the organic content, the darker the shale's color.

Burgess Shale
Shales are an excellent place to find fossils, and those found in the Burgess Shale in Canada are exceptional. They date from the Cambrian period, 505 million years ago, and are beautifully preserved. This fossil is one of largest arthropods found there.

Slate
If shale is compressed and heated, it may metamorphose into slate (see pages 148–149). Slate usually forms from sedimentary rock.

SHALE SAMPLES

Oil shale

Red shale

Shale slab

Monterey shale
A rib-shaped shale formation stretches offshore from northern to southern California. Known as the Monterey Formation, it is a 1,700-square-mile (4,440 sq km) area of oil- and gas-bearing shale that contains an estimated 15 billion barrels of oil.

FOSSIL GALLERY

Fossils are the petrified remains of plants, and dead animals, their footprints, trackways and burrows. They have been preserved in rock formed from the mud or sand they were buried in. They are our only evidence of long-extinct creatures such as dinosaurs.

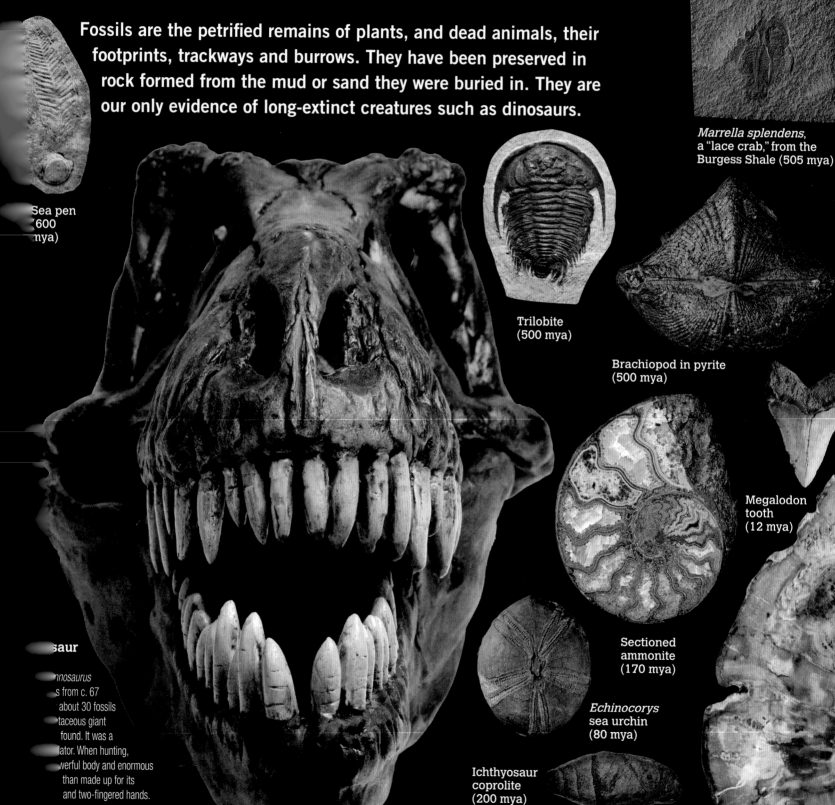

Sea pen (600 mya)

Marrella splendens, a "lace crab," from the Burgess Shale (505 mya)

Trilobite (500 mya)

Brachiopod in pyrite (500 mya)

Megalodon tooth (12 mya)

Sectioned ammonite (170 mya)

Echinocorys sea urchin (80 mya)

Ichthyosaur coprolite (200 mya)

...saur

...nnosaurus
...s from c. 67
...about 30 fossils
...taceous giant
...found. It was a
...ator. When hunting,
...werful body and enormous
...than made up for its
...and two-fingered hands.

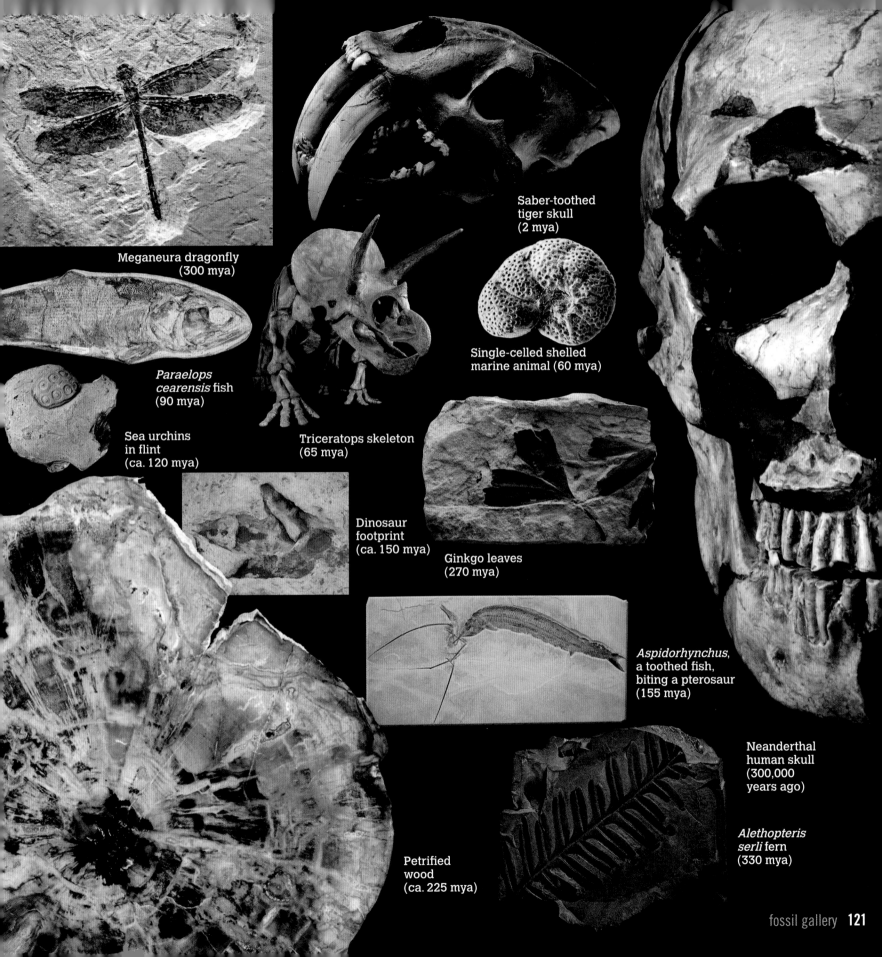

Meganeura dragonfly
(300 mya)

Saber-toothed
tiger skull
(2 mya)

*Paraelops
cearensis* fish
(90 mya)

Single-celled shelled
marine animal (60 mya)

Sea urchins
in flint
(ca. 120 mya)

Triceratops skeleton
(65 mya)

Dinosaur
footprint
(ca. 150 mya)

Ginkgo leaves
(270 mya)

Aspidorhynchus,
a toothed fish,
biting a pterosaur
(155 mya)

Neanderthal
human skull
(300,000
years ago)

Petrified
wood
(ca. 225 mya)

*Alethopteris
serli* fern
(330 mya)

SANDSTONE

SEDIMENTARY CLASTIC ROCK

Sandstone is a common rock used in many buildings and monuments. It is less resistant than most limestones and granites, as can be seen in cemeteries where old sandstone monuments are often the most eroded. It comes from deserts, rivers, and seas and forms stone of an array of colors, including dramatic reds and yellows.

Brownstone houses
New York City has rows of houses that are known as brownstones. These are either made of or have facades of reddish-brown sandstone. It was a popular stone because it was easy to work, so it could have varied ornate designs.

Rock type: sedimentary

Main locations: sedimentary basins around the world

Major minerals: over 95 percent quartz grains; but can also be rich in feldspar, calcite, mica, and clay minerals

Color: many colors, from black and beige through green and gray to pink, white, and yellow; red when of desert origin

Form: sandy grains that are often smooth and rounded

Texture: medium to coarse grained

Weather impact: poor to good resistance

Uses: buildings; sand; glassmaking; grinding stones

SANDSTONE SAMPLES

Green sandstone

Quartzite

Ferruginous sandstone

Weathered sandstone

Millet-seed sandstone

Desert stone
The grains in sandstone have usually been reduced in size by weathering, then moved to a different site by water, wind, or ice. Then, over time, they turn to layered stone. The pipes in this pipe-rock quartzite are probably the burrows of ancient animals.

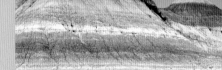

Painting the desert
The well-named Painted Desert sits on a plateau in Arizona and covers 7,500 square miles (19,400 sq km). Its brilliantly colored layers of sandstones, marls, and shales turn the long stretch of badland hills into a wonderfully rainbow-colored landscape.

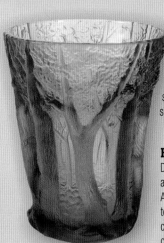

Glass production

Sand has been used in glassmaking for thousands of years. In about 3000 BCE, in ancient Egypt, melted sand was used to make glass beads. Today, sandstone that has at least 98 percent silica is used for high-quality glassware.

Rose-red Petra

Deep in the Jordanian desert between the Red and Dead Seas is the "rose-red city" of Petra. At its height, around 50 CE, the city was home to 20,000 people. It is carved out of vividly colored sandstone cliff faces and marks the crossroads of ancient trading routes.

Sandstone and gneiss

Millions of years ago, under great heat and pressure deep inside Earth, sandstone metamorphosed into gneiss (see page 145). The minerals recrystallized and separated into alternating layers.

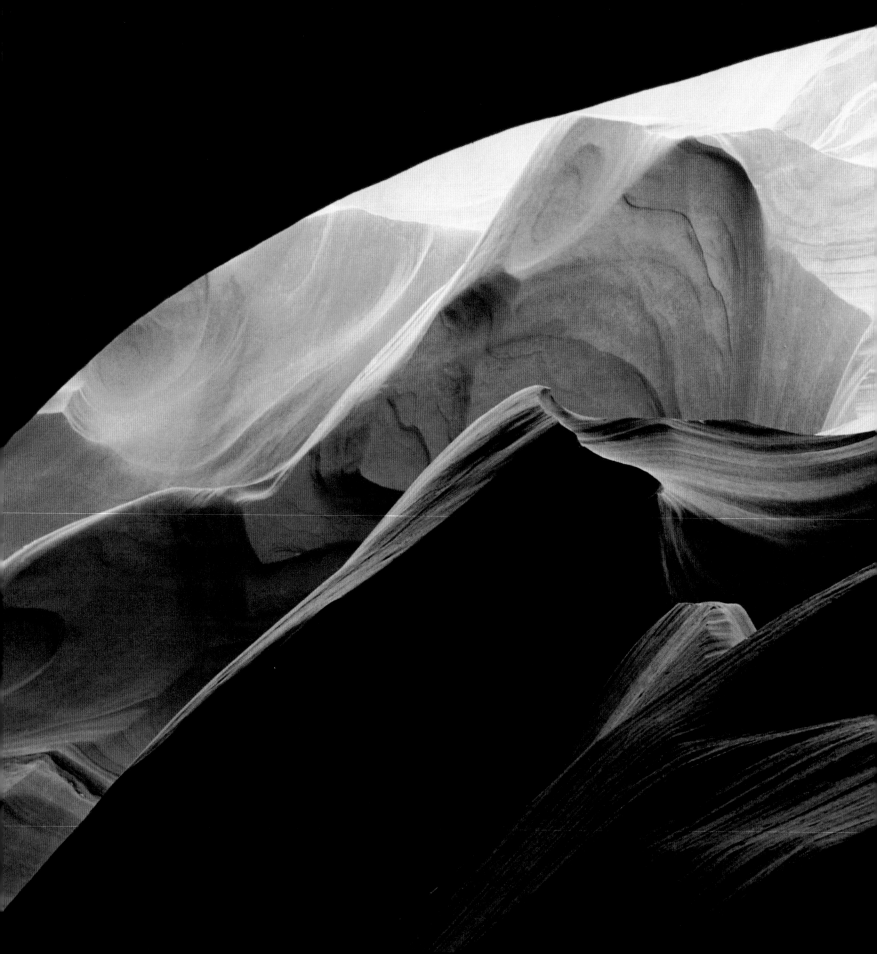

Sandstone canyon

This narrow slot canyon in Arizona was formed by the rushing of seasonal flash floods (from thunderstorms) through sandstone. The water finds hairline cracks in the sandstone, eventually cutting natural arches, holes, and curves with the abrasive particles of sand that it picks up as it swirls along. These narrow gorges are much deeper than they are wide, and they twist and turn, sometimes letting in light to show off the sandstone's wonderful colors. Some hollows are very deep and let in only glimmers of light.

TUFA

CALCIUM CARBONATE

Tufa is an oddity. It builds up around the rims of calcite-rich springs, just like lime scale coats our baths and taps. The rock grows where lime-rich waters flow, so it might coat a cliff or waterfall, form a crust over mosses and other plants, or even grow into underwater towers.

TUFA SAMPLES

Calcareous tufa

Calcareous tufa

Travertine

Calcareous tufa

Layered tufa

Rock type: sedimentary, limestone

Main locations: in limestone areas; near hot springs, lakes, and geysers

Major minerals: calcite; occasionally aragonite

Color: white, cream, yellow; often stained brown to red by iron oxides

Form: masses, occasionally banded, stalactites and stalagmites, sometimes botryoidal; tufa is porous; travertine is compacted form

Texture: compact to earthy; crumbles

Weather impact: fairly resistant

Uses: building materials; sculptures; casting medium for jewelry; molds (tufa does not crack or distort)

Tufa landscape

The thermal pools of Pamukkale—the name means "Cotton Palace"—in Turkey are an incredible tourist attraction. The calcium carbonate shelves filled with warm, milky-blue water inspired the ancient Romans to build a spa town. It is now a UNESCO World Heritage Site.

Tufa rock

Tufa s a highly porous sedimentary rock that is formed by the evaporation of water. This process results in a coarse stone that is irregular in shape and full of holes.

Mono Lake

Up to 2 million birds feed and rest in California's Mono Lake each year, but the lake is remarkable for another reason. For over 1 million years, salts and minerals have washed into the lake and been left behind as the freshwater evaporated. Today, spectacular tufa pinnacles have been left exposed because the water level has fallen.

Rock network

The rapid evaporation of freshwater sometimes gives tufa a fibrous appearance. This close-up of the surface shows many hollows that were probably left when organic matter decomposed.

Petrifying well

In 1630, a "Petrifying Well" outside Mother Shipton's Cave in Yorkshire, England, was opened to the public. Since then, objects such as this teddy bear have been turned to stone by the tufa deposited around the well.

Colosseum stone

The Romans built a special 12-mile (20 km) road from Tibur (now Tivoli) to carry mined tufa to Rome. The stone was used for the main pillars, the ground floor, and the external wall of the Colosseum, which was inaugurated in 80 CE.

ROCK SALT

SODIUM CHLORIDE

If you want to dry out a body before you mummify it, or make food last longer and taste better, or even get rid of the slippery ice on a road, you need rock salt. It forms where salty water from seas or lakes dries out; it is also mined underground. This is a rock that we eat regularly, and it is very important for our health.

Rock type: sedimentary, marine, evaporite

Main locations: arid areas where seawater or lake water has evaporated; deposits buried in ancient rock

Major minerals: halite

Color: colorless, white when pure; also yellow, gray, black, brown, red

Form: masses of interlocking cubic crystals; sometimes octahedral crystals, grains

Texture: coarsely crystalline

Weather impact: soluble in water

Uses: table salt; soaps; glazes for porcelain; enamel; baking soda; caustic soda; road gritting; water-softening

ROCK SALT SAMPLES

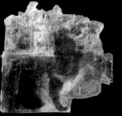

Rock salt with blue inclusion

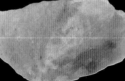

Himalayan pink rock salt

Salar de Uyuni
This is the world's largest salt flat. The glistening white sand extends over 4,085 square miles (10,580 sq km) in southwestern Bolivia. Up to 70 percent of the world's lithium reserves may be underneath the salt surface, in large reservoirs of lithium-rich brine.

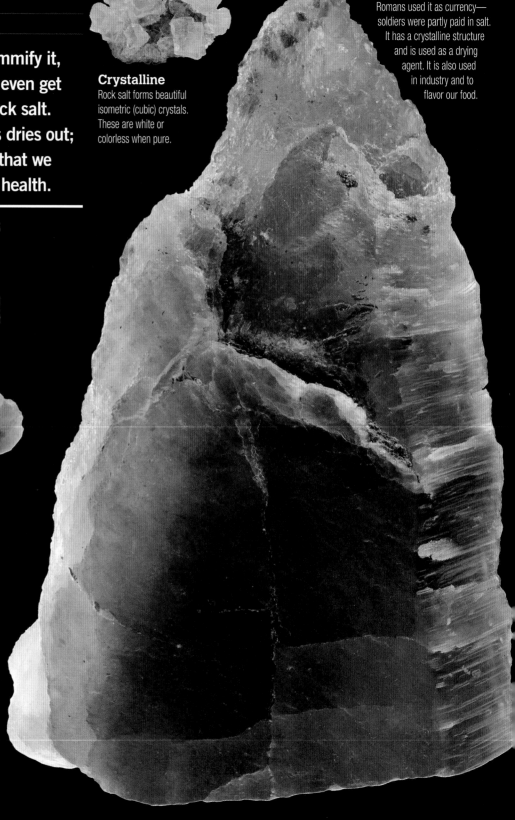

Crystalline
Rock salt forms beautiful isometric (cubic) crystals. These are white or colorless when pure.

Rock salt
This soft rock is mined for its pure form, halite. The ancient Romans used it as currency—soldiers were partly paid in salt. It has a crystalline structure and is used as a drying agent. It is also used in industry and to flavor our food.

ROCK GYPSUM

SEDIMENTARY GYPSUM

Also known as gyprock, rock gypsum has been called "the rock that nobody knows," because few people are aware of how widely it is used. This rock is the main source for the mineral gypsum, which is used to make drywall for building, in foods, to improve soil, and to set broken limbs. So now you know all about rock gypsum!

Rock type: sedimentary, marine, evaporite sediments

Main locations: saltwater lakes, salt flats; buried deposits often with sandstone, mudstone, or limestone

Major minerals: gypsum and anhydrite; lesser amounts of calcite, dolomite, clay minerals, limonite

Color: colorless, white, brownish

Form: simple tabular crystals, often with curved faces; aggregates, fibrous or granular masses; twins are common

Texture: coarsely crystalline

Weather impact: not resistant

Uses: filler in paper and textiles; plaster of Paris; plaster and drywall; cement manufacturing; decorative plasterwork; plaster casts; blackboard chalk

ROCK GYPSUM SAMPLES

Gypsum crystals

Rock gypsum

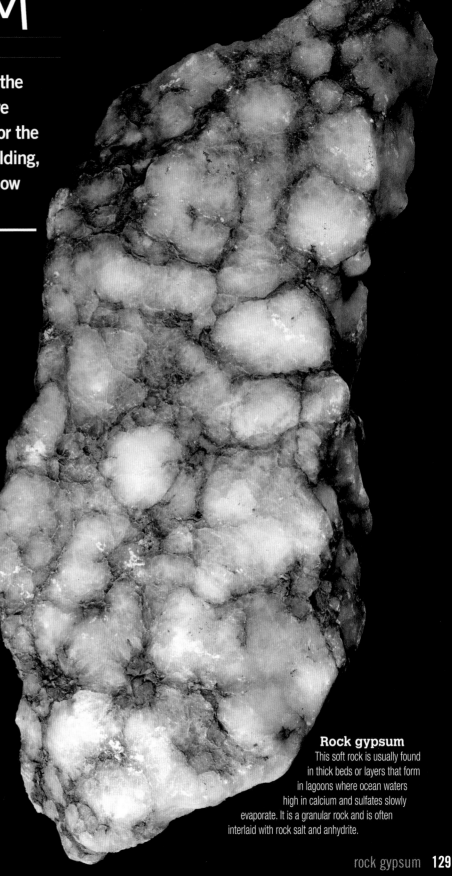

Rock gypsum
This soft rock is usually found in thick beds or layers that form in lagoons where ocean waters high in calcium and sulfates slowly evaporate. It is a granular rock and is often interlaid with rock salt and anhydrite.

White sands
Covering a huge area of 275 square miles (710 sq km) in New Mexico, this vast desert is full of spectacular dunes of pure white gypsum.

Desert rose
Gypsum crystallizes in the most surprising rosette patterns. These desert roses form in only tens to hundreds of years. It is said that if you find one, you will be blessed with good luck.

MORE SEDIMENTARY ROCKS

Some sedimentary rock bursts with life—or what was once alive. This might be the fossils of plants and animals that lived on land or in the oceans millions of years ago, or it could be plants that died in swampy areas and turned first to peat, then coal.

Flint with urchin fossil

Halite (rock salt)

Chert

Sandstone

Diatomite formed from diatom fossils

Stalactite section

Kukerite oil shale

Phosphorite

Shale

Cambrian blue clay

Conglomerate

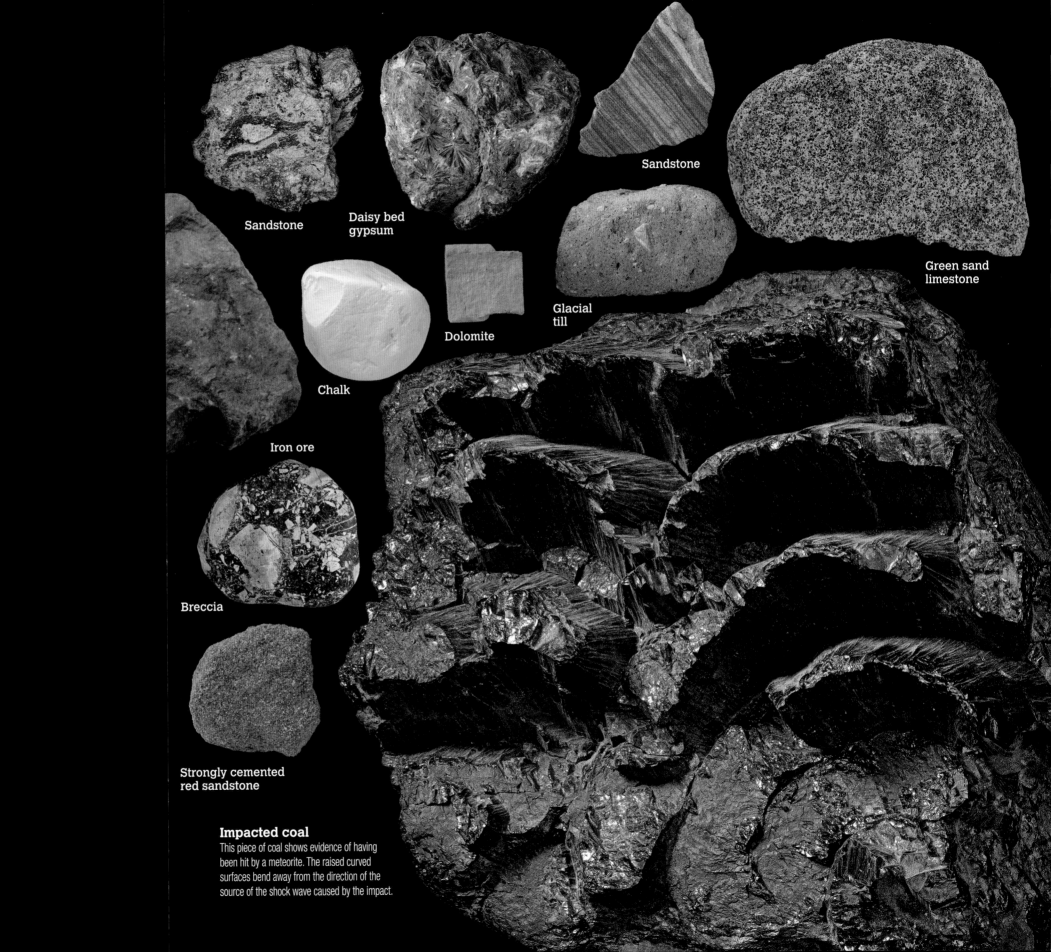

Sandstone

Daisy bed gypsum

Sandstone

Green sand limestone

Chalk

Dolomite

Glacial till

Iron ore

Breccia

Strongly cemented red sandstone

Impacted coal
This piece of coal shows evidence of having been hit by a meteorite. The raised curved surfaces bend away from the direction of the source of the shock wave caused by the impact.

COAL

ORGANIC SEDIMENTARY ROCK

It has been worn as jewelry, shoveled to power steam trains, and ground to powder to make filters to purify water . . . and it is still burned today to make electricity. Coal isn't a mineral, because it came from living things—rotting leaves, seeds, and dead wood that got buried, then naturally compressed and heated to become first peat, then brittle black rock.

Rock type: sedimentary, chemical

Main locations: in rock strata in layers

Major minerals: various amounts of bitumen, clay minerals, quartz, pyrite, calcite; with graphite in highest grade of coal

Color: black, brown, gray

Form: veins or pebbles; breaks into hard, bright rectangular lumps

Texture: hard, bright lumps

Weather impact: fairly resistant

Uses: home fires; electricity production; steel production; soaps; aspirins; solvents; dyes; plastics; rayon; nylon; filters for water; silicon metal, used to produce lubricants, water repellents, resins, cosmetics, shampoos, and toothpastes

Coal seams

Coal usually formed in a swamp environment. Plant debris fell into the swamp, and the standing water kept it from decaying quickly because of the lack of oxygen. This means that when coal is found, it is often in seams between layers of older and younger rocks.

Ancient coal forests

This fossil was once part of a tall tree that flourished in a forest 325 million years ago. It is the fossilized roots of *Stigmaria ficoides*, a type of lycopod tree found in ancient coal forests during the Carboniferous period.

COAL SAMPLES

Coal showing meteorite impact

Bituminous coal

Lignite

Bituminous coal

Anthracite

Different types of coal contain different amounts of carbon. Anthracite (right) contains more than 92 percent. Sometimes called "hard" coal, anthracite formed from bituminous (or "soft") coal when high pressures developed during deep burial or mountain-building episodes. This naturally occurring, smokeless fuel is very shiny, hard, and dense, and it burns extremely slowly, with a high heat output.

FOSSIL FUELS

Coal is one of the natural fuels that formed in prehistoric times from the remains of plants and animals. These fossil fuels include oil and gas in addition to coal; we burn them to power industry and our homes. However, they are nonrenewable, so we are looking for alternatives.

1940s coal mining
Coal is usually buried deep underground, so a network of rooms or tunnels is cut into a coal seam. These were originally mined by hand (above). Although miners today use modern equipment, it can be very dangerous work.

Opencut mining
Mining in this way is economic only when a coal seam is near the surface. Large opencut mines can cover vast areas and use very large machinery. The world's largest two-axle dump truck is being used to transport coal in opencut mines in Siberia.

Nodding donkey
On land, a pump jack, or nodding donkey, can be used if there is not enough pressure to cause oil to flow all the way to the surface. The pump jack can bring up to 10.5 gallons (40 L) with one "nod."

Oil rig
Crude oil and gas were created over millions of years, from huge amounts of microscopic plankton that formed layers on the seabed and were covered by mud. Today, oil companies use oil rigs to drill into the seabed and bring up the oil and gas.

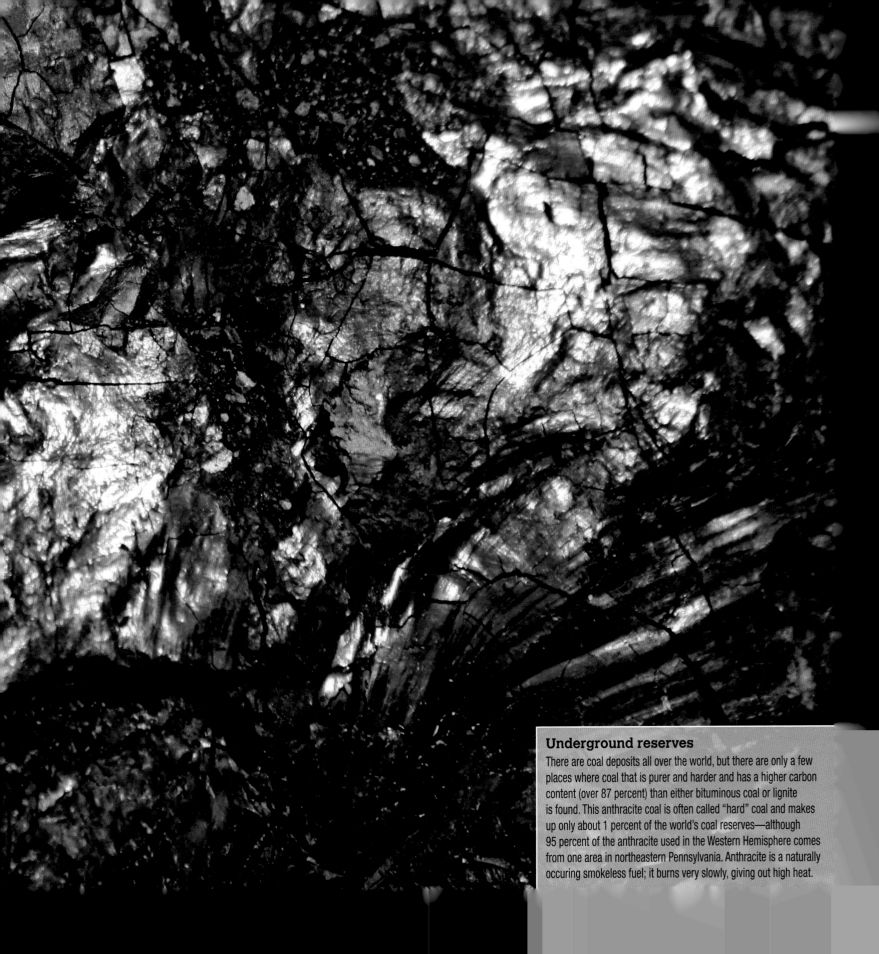

Underground reserves

There are coal deposits all over the world, but there are only a few places where coal that is purer and harder and has a higher carbon content (over 87 percent) than either bituminous coal or lignite is found. This anthracite coal is often called "hard" coal and makes up only about 1 percent of the world's coal reserves—although 95 percent of the anthracite used in the Western Hemisphere comes from one area in northeastern Pennsylvania. Anthracite is a naturally occuring smokeless fuel; it burns very slowly, giving out high heat.

FLINT

SEDIMENTARY CHERT

Flint has been used to make **tools** and **weapons** for **3 million** years.

Flint takes us back in time to when early people discovered that its hard, sharp flakes made the best cutting tools and weapons. They also struck flint to create sparks to light fires. Today it is sometimes used for building houses, because it weathers much better than most other stones.

Rock type: sedimentary, marine

Main locations: in existing chalk rocks; can concentrate in layers within the chalk

Major minerals: quartz or chalcedony

Color: black, brown, green, gray, blue-gray, red, yellow, white

Form: nodules and masses in chalks and limestones

Texture: microcrystalline

Weather impact: resistant

Uses: grinding agent for ceramic and paint industries; building material; lighting fires; making roads

FLINT SAMPLES

Flint nodule

Banded flint

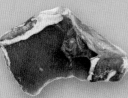
Glassy flint

Echinoids in flint

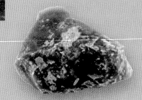
Weathered flint

Rocky rivers
Flint is a rocky feature of some riverbeds. The Pedernales River, which winds for more than 105 miles (170 km) through central Texas before flowing into the Colorado River (above), is even named for the rock. *Pedernales* comes from the Spanish word for flint.

Sharp glass
Flint is hard but is easily split into thin plates that have a glassy or pearly appearance. It usually has a curved but even surface, with sharp edges.

Lighting up

Flint is a very hard form of rock. If you strike iron or steel with flint, the flint flakes off tiny particles of iron. The force of the blow and the friction it creates ignite the iron, and it burns. The sparks from this lighter are the iron burning.

Hagstone

Some flints have natural holes through them. Many people believed that these could ward off witches, sickness, and nightmares. They also looked through them to "see" invisible spirits!

Flint arrowhead

The hard, sharp edges of flint make it very useful for weaponry. Native Americans made arrowheads and other weapons from bone, horn, or stones such as flint.

Egyptian knife

From the earliest times, razor-sharp flint has been used as a cutting tool. This ancient Egyptian flint knife was used to cut up meat for food and prepare animal skins to use as leather.

Flintlock pistol, 1700s

Flintlock pistols were in common use for more than 200 years, starting in the 1600s. A powerful spring struck a flint to make a spark that lit gunpowder. The resulting explosion fired bullets out through the barrel.

METAMORPHIC ROCKS

These rocks began as igneous or sedimentary rocks that were heated deep beneath Earth's surface, often under mountains or volcanoes. They twisted and bent and took in new minerals. "Cooked" into new rocks such as marble, slate, or jade, they were pushed up to the surface by the movement of Earth's plates.

Cararra marble

Gneiss

Biotite schist with almandine garnet

Pink marble

Quartzite with cubic quartz and pyrite

Mica schist

Serpentinite

Marbleized hornfels

Monte Rosa gneiss

Gneiss

Marble

Marble is metamorphosed limestone or dolomite. These rocks are often found among other metamorphic rocks such as grneiss and mica schist.

Quartzite

Quartzite

Slate with pyrite

Marble pebble

Schist

Red aventurine quartzite

Calcic skarn

Ferruginous-quartzite

Jaspilite

Hornfel with long andalusite crystals

Migmatite

Schist

Silver schist with garnets

MARBLE
METAMORPHOSED LIMESTONE

Marble is a proud stone—it seems to glow from within, and it was carved into countless statues in classical Greek and Roman times. It forms out of limestone and is naturally creamy white, but impurities add all sorts of shades. It is soft enough to carve but withstands most weather.

Rock type: metamorphic, regional, contact

Main locations: mountain-building areas worldwide

Major minerals: calcite, dolomite; may contain garnet, talc, amphibole, pyroxende, olivine, wollastonite

Color: white, pink, red, blue-gray, green, brown, black

Form: often masses; can be banded; may have sedimentary bedding

Texture: fine to coarse grained

Weather impact: resistant

Uses: sculptures; monuments; flooring and tiles; crushed for aggregates; powdered for whitewash, cosmetics, paper, fillers, putty

Color and pattern
Marble varies considerably in both color and pattern. The swirls and "veins" of many marbles are caused by impurities in the original limestone. Grains of quartz or maybe micas react with the dolomite in the original limestone during metamorphism. New minerals form as the earlier ones become unstable.

MARBLE SAMPLES

Grossular (garnet) marble

Diopside (pyroxene) marble

Green layered marble

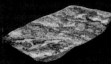

Foliated marble

Phlogopite (mica) saccharoidal marble

Green-and-white marble

Marble, CO
The town of Marble in Colorado gets its name from the Yule Marble Quarry, which operated from 1905 to 1941. It was the source of the marble that was used for the exterior of the Lincoln Memorial in Washington, D.C. Yule marble was adopted as the state rock of Colorado in 2004.

Taj Mahal

Marble has been used for some extraordinary building projects, and there is no more amazing structure than this mausoleum of white marble in Agra, India. It was built from 1631 to 1648 by 20,000 workers and 1,000 elephants by order of Shah Jahan, in memory of his favorite wife, Mumtaz Mahal. The different types of marble came from many countries, including China, Afghanistan, Sri Lanka, and Saudi Arabia.

CARVING IN MARBLE

Maybe the most popular material used for sculpture, marble is translucent and durable. This may be why it has been the choice of all the greatest sculptors, from Greek artist Phidias (ca. 490–430 BCE) to Michelangelo (1475–1564) and Bernini (1598–1680) to Rodin (1840–1917).

Cycladic figure

This curiously modern-looking statue was created 4,500 years ago on the Cyclades, a group of islands off the coast of Greece. The only facial feature carved in the white marble of this statue is the nose.

Italian marble

Where marble occurs, it can be hundreds of yards thick, so it is quarried on a large scale. One of the most famous areas for quarries is at Carrara, Italy, in the Apuan Alps.

Work of genius

The quarries of Carrara are the source of some of the most famous statues in the world, including Michelangelo's *David*. Created between 1501 and 1504, the 17-foot-tall (5.2 m) statue was carved from a single block of marble.

Lincoln Memorial

In 1922, a memorial honoring the "Great Emancipator" and 16th president of the United States, Abraham Lincoln, opened to the public. The statue is 19 feet (5.8 m) high and weighs 175 tons. It is carved from 28 blocks of white Georgia marble.

Rock of many faces

Marble is a granular rock with a mass of interlocking calcite or dolomite crystals. It is usually very light in color; at its purest, it is a bright white. Because its crystalline structure is firm, marble can be polished to a high sheen.

Natural wonder

The Catedral de Mármol (the Marble Cathedral) is part of a spectacular series of caverns on the northern shore of the Lago General Carrera, in a wild and inaccessible area of Patagonia, on the border between Chile and Argentina. The water-sculpted blue caverns reflect the light of the azure waters of one of South America's largest and deepest freshwater lakes. Over the last 6,000 years, silt in the glacial waters from great ice fields and nearby glaciers has carved fantastically labyrinthine shapes out of a peninsula of solid marble.

SCHIST

MEDIUM GRADE METAMORPHIC ROCK

Schist is slate's shiny cousin. Both of them form from clay or mud, and both have layers of platey minerals and break into sheets. However, schist forms at higher temperatures and pressures than slate does (see pages 148–149), so it has larger crystals, making it look shinier and more silvery.

Rock type: metamorphic, regional

Main locations: mountain-building areas worldwide

Major minerals: muscovite, biotite, chlorite, quartz; may also contain garnet, kyanite, staurolite

Color: silver, gray, green, brown, blue, gray, black; sometimes sparkling

Form: often alternates lighter and darker bands; often shiny; visible crystals that line up to form a schistosity

Texture: medium grained

Weather impact: resistant

Uses: decorative rock walls; jewelry; buildings; fireplaces; patios; insecticides; potting soil mixes

Schist in the landscape

The word *schist* comes from the ancient Greek for "split." In landscapes such as this one at Kriyyy Rih in Ukraine, the rock has been tilted, clearly revealing its many layers. The rock has a tendency to split, a quality known as schistosity.

Staurolite schist

Schist forms in such heat and pressure that it allows for the creation of new minerals, such as garnet, kyanite, and staurolite. Its large crystals reflect light, so it is shiny.

Manhattan

This famous island is built on Manhattan schist. The rock forms a spine from the Henry Hudson Bridge in the north to the Battery at the southern tip. It is not the only metamorphic rock in the area—marble runs under the East River, and gneiss surfaces in the Bronx.

Migmatite

This rock forms at temperatures that partially melt the rock. The first parts to melt are the quartz and feldspar. These can collect and move through the rock to crystallize in the form of veins. Migmatites form in both gneiss and schist.

Biotite schist with mauve garnet

Hornblende schist

Silver schist with garnets

GNEISS

HIGH GRADE METAMORPHIC ROCK

Gneiss is the granddaddy of rocks. The oldest-known rock on the planet is a 3.9-million-year-old lump of gneiss found in Canada. Gneiss survives because it is tough, and does not split along planes of weakness like most metamorphic rocks do. Gneiss can form from igneous, sedimentary, or preexisting metamorphic rocks.

Rock type: metamorphic, regional

Main locations: widespread, especially in lower parts of the continental crust; associated with mountain building

Major minerals: feldspars and quartz in light-colored bands; biotite, augite, and hornblende in dark-colored bands; may contain garnets, staurolite, sillimanite

Color: white, red, pink, brown, black

Form: granular appearance; may show alternating dark and light bands; sometimes folded

Texture: coarse grained

Weather impact: resistant

Uses: cladding for buildings, pavements, road construction

Stone of pharaohs
The ancient Egyptians built statues to last. This majestic enthroned sculpture is of the pharaoh Khafre, who ruled ca. 2520– 2494 BCE. It is made of diorite gneiss quarried from Gebel el-Asr, the only quarry in Egypt that produced three varieties of the much-prized metamorphic rock.

Washington Monument
This obelisk, finished in 1884, towers 555 feet (169 m) above the National Mall in Washington, D.C. It is made of Maryland blue gneiss and Maine granite, and faced with white marble.

GNEISS SAMPLES

Gneiss with pink feldspar "augen" ("eyes")

Monte Rosa gneiss

Sparkling rock
Gneiss has wavy dark and light bands of separated minerals where the rocks have folded under pressure. Its name is German, meaning "spark," because it contains sparkly chunks of quartz and feldspar. In this sample there are blue kyanite and reddish-brown staurolite.

Dark dikes
On the island of Guernsey in the English Channel, there are sheetlike formations known as the Icart Gneiss. The dark bands are crystallized magma that intruded into the gneiss after it formed. The lighter gneiss contrasts with these dark bands, which are called dikes.

QUARTZITE
QUARTZ-RICH METAMORPHIC ROCK

Quartzite causes trouble. It is so hard that geologists are warned to take extra care if they have to hit it with hammers, and its use in construction is limited because it damages the equipment. This strength comes from its pattern of interlocking quartz grains.

Rock type: metamorphic, regional, contact

Main locations: in areas formed during mountain-building events; as a contact metamorphic rock next to igneous intrusions

Major minerals: mostly quartz; sometimes feldspar, mica, hematite

Color: snowy white, pink, gray

Form: masses; may show evidence of original sandstone

Texture: fine to medium grained

Weather impact: resistant

Uses: bricks and other building materials; decorative stone; crushed for aggregates; armor for seawalls; paving; building facings; railway ballast; countertops; statues; monuments; jewelry

Tougher than the rest

When quartz-rich sandstone is heated under pressure, it recrystallizes in a different form. This creates interlocking quartz grains and results in one of the toughest rocks on Earth.

Carved in stone

Quartzite was a popular stone for statues in ancient Egypt. Pharaohs such as Amenhotep III had enormous quartzite statues erected in temples. This quartzite statue, however, is a private sculpture commissioned around 1850–1830 bce by an official called Ankhrekhu.

Golden rock

Gold can occur in unexpected places—for example, in quartzite deposits. Quartzite that is glassy in appearance can contain as much as 70 ounces (1,980 g) of gold per ton.

QUARTZITE SAMPLES

Quartzite rock

Banded quartzite

Sioux cliffs

The Sioux quartzite cliffs rise 100 feet (30 m) from the plains in Blue Mounds State Park in Minnesota. Nearly 1 billion years ago, the quartzite was part of an entire mountain range of quartzite that stretched from southwestern Minnesota to central South Dakota. Today, some of the quartzite is exposed in outcrops like this.

FULGURITE

FUSED QUARTZ SAND

Fulgurite has been called "petrified energy" and "lightning stone" because this rock is made when lightning strikes sand or rock. This heats the ground enough to melt it, leaving a stone that has a rough outer surface and a smooth, glassy interior. Gas bubbles trapped inside can give clues to the world as it was millions of years ago.

Rock type: metamorphic, contact

Main locations: desert regions and rocky areas where there are lightning strikes

Major minerals: amorphous silica

Color: white to pale gray and shiny black

Form: sand fulgurites are tubular, with a glassy interior and sandy exterior, or crusty, with branches stretching out from the center; rock fulgurites are where the surface of a rock melts

Texture: glassy; tubes in sand may have sandy surfaces of unfused quartz grains

Weather impact: resistant

Uses: collectors' items

FULGURITE SAMPLES

Crusty fulgurite

Glassy fulgurite with hollowed center

Desert lightning

Most fulgurites are found in desert regions where sand has been melted. A bolt of lightning with a temperature of 7,200°F (4,000°C) hits the ground, fusing the sand, which has a melting point of 3,100°F (1,700°C).

Tektite

Other glass objects are also formed by impact and heat. They are called tektites. When a large meteorite hits Earth, it can melt the rock that it lands on. The molten rock is hurled into the air, cooling quickly to form glass. Tektites are usually found in "strewn fields" related to specific impact craters.

Fulgurite

Fulgurites form as crusts or tubes. Sometimes they have many branches that trace the zigzagging paths of the lightning bolts that formed them.

SLATE

FOLIATED METAMORPHIC ROCK

Slate has a split personality. It forms from fine-grained mudstone, shale or volcanic tuff. During metamorphism, its platy crystals reorientate and grow so that they lie at right angles to the source of pressure. This means that the slate splits perfectly along parallel surfaces, which are called planes of cleavage.

Rock type: metamorphic, regional

Main locations: in areas formed during mountain-building events

Major minerals: chlorite, biotite, muscovite, quartz, sometimes pyrite

Color: black, green, red, brown, purple

Form: smooth; shows well-developed slatey cleavage; often mottled or spotted by contact metamorphism

Texture: very fine grained

Weather impact: resistant

Uses: flooring; roofing; paving; tabletops; in early electric panels and switch boxes (slate is a good electrical insulator)

Slate
This dense and fine-grained rock is usually quite dull in appearance, although it sometimes sparkles with micas. This slate was formed when volcanic ash was deposited in water and then metamorphosed.

SLATE SAMPLES

Red slate

Pale gray slate

Dark gray slate with pyrite

Slate mountains

Around 70 CE, the Romans first took slate from the mountains around Llanberis, in northern Wales, to build their fort on the outskirts of today's Caernarvon. Later, the slate was used by medieval castle builders. By the 1870s, commercial mines were flourishing all over this area.

Deformed fossils

Intensely metamorphosed rocks do not contain fossils, because they are completely destroyed in the metamorphic process. Slate is an exception, because the process is not as violent and some fossils survive. However, they can become flattened and squeezed, or stretched completely out of shape. Unlike many, this fossil (above) is recognizable, as a trilobite (right).

Classroom slates

Slate can be written on and wiped clean, so it was ideal in early classrooms. These teaching aids were most popular worldwide during the 19th century but are still used in some countries today.

Towering mine waste

Vast amounts of waste from slate mining loom behind houses at Blaenau Ffestiniog, in northern Wales. This was the location of the largest slate mine in the world, where tens of thousands of tons of slate were produced in the 19th and 20th centuries.

Film clapboard

Slate is the material traditionally used for clapboards in the filmmaking industry. A clapboard displaying scene information is held in front of the camera, for easy identification by the film editor later.

Black slate pavement

In Lugo, Spain, on the Bay of Biscay, wind and seawater have carved vaults, arches, galleries, and caverns in the slate of the cliffs. Whistles of wind filter through the holes and chimneys, sounding like the notes of a giant organ. At the beach called Playa de Aguas Santas, rocky strata of black slate dating from the early Ordovician period (488–444 million years ago) reach 100 feet (30 m) high in places. About 90 percent of Europe's natural roofing slate is produced and exported by quarries in Spain.

HORNFELS
THERMAL METAMORPHIC ROCK

When magma rises or squeezes into Earth's crust, its heat bakes the rocks around it. This softens the rocks, making them recrystallize and sometimes even grow new minerals. Where the heat is most intense, the rock becomes fine-grained, with interlocking and randomly oriented crystals. Tough, splintery hornfels is born.

Looking closer
Under the microscope, the structure of hornfels is distinctive, with small, equally sized grains interlocking snugly like the pieces of a mosaic. This is because the rock was heated to a high temperature. The minerals changed, but they did not develop new banding.

Rock type: metamorphic, contact

Main locations: next to intrusions (dykes, sills, batholiths) or below lava flows in high-temperature, low-pressure environments

Major minerals: chlorite, muscovite, biotite, quartz; sometimes andalusite, cordierite when formed from shale or slate

Color: gray, brown, black

Form: banded zones immediately next to igneous rocks

Texture: fine to coarse grained

Weather impact: resistant

Uses: aggregates for roads and construction; decorative elements; artifacts; monuments

HORNFELS SAMPLES

Spotted hornfels

Hornfels with long andalusite crystals

Siliceous hornfels

Cordierite hornfels

Striped cliffs
Near Hagi, Japan, is a colorful and banded stretch of coast called the Susa Hornfels. The cliffs—striped in black, white, and ash brown—have been designated a Japanese natural monument. The striped pattern of the Susa cliffs is called *tatami-ishi* in Japanese.

Contact metamorphism
When magma pushes its way through Earth's crust along cracks in a rock formation it cools to form an igneous intrusion. Although the rock in the intrusion is igneous, the rock the magma contacts may be metamorphized. This has happened here with the darker-colored igneous rock diabase and metamorphic hornfels.

Rock band
In 1890, an unusual concert took place in New Jersey. The Till family, from the Lake District in England, played stone xylophones made from "Skiddaw stone," a type of hornfels with great tone quality and resonance. Bars of the stone were supported on wooden stands. The heaviest instruments weighed more than 1.5 tons.

Horn rock
The name *hornfels* comes from the German for "horn rock," because the rock's edges are semitransparent like animal horn. This is a hard, flinty, fine-grained rock formed by contact metamorphism. It recrystallizes with an altered texture.

AMPHIBOLITE

METAMORPHIC BASALTIC ROCK

Amphibolite is one of the toughest rocks, because it is formed under pressure and heat that transform even the softest sediments into resilient schists and gneisses. This makes it harder than limestone and heavier than granite, so it is ideal for construction use in road building and railroad ballast.

Rock type: metamorphic, regional

Main locations: mountain ranges, plate boundaries, deep oceanic crust

Major minerals: mainly hornblende; sometimes with actinolite and plagioclase feldspar; may contain garnet or epidote

Color: gray, black, green

Form: shiny (from the hornblende), weakly foliated; sometimes dark and light bands

Texture: medium to coarse grained

Weather impact: resistant

Uses: aggregrates for road building; railway ballast; construction; paving; building facings; countertops; ornaments; jewelry, especially beads; paperweights; bookends

AMPHIBOLITE SAMPLES

Amphibolite

Pale gray amphibolite

Pale green epidotite in hornblende schist

Chynov Cave

Discovered in 1863 by workers in a quarry, this became the first Czech cave to be opened to the public. The swirling, lighter-colored layers of marble are offset by the dark amphibolite fillings in between. Sometimes the two rocks create "eyes"—circular shapes in the walls. The steep corridors lead down to a depth of 135 feet (41 m).

Speckled stone

This amphibolite is rich with red garnets. The salt-and-pepper appearance comes from the white of plagioclase feldspar and the black of hornblende.

ECLOGITE

BASALTIC METAMORPHIC ROCK

Eclogites are rare and beautiful green and red rocks. They have the same chemical composition as basalt, but have formed at enormous depths, and contain denser minerals. Some eclogites contain diamonds, which form at depths of over 60 miles (100 km). How they reach the surface? Geologists cannot agree.

Rock type: metamorphic, regional

Main locations: may be brought to the surface near present-day subduction zones, as xenoliths in basalt, or kimberlite pipes

Major minerals: garnet, the pyroxene omphacite; may contain diamond, kyanite, zoisite, quartz, rutile, coesite

Color: red, green

Form: as blocks in melange; as bands or lenses in gneisses, as xenoliths

Texture: medium to coarse grained

Weather impact: resistant

Uses: dike construction; jewelry; source of diamonds, garnets, and other semiprecious stones; collectors' items; buildings; facings; countertops; paving; aggregates

Christmas rock

No other rock is so full of unusual crystals and minerals—eclogite is sometimes called "Christmas rock" because it is scattered with bright green, red, and white minerals. It is usually rich in red garnets, like this sample is.

Rich in minerals

Eclogites contain other minerals, including omphacite, carinthine, kyanite, lawsonite, and zoisite. This rock is also very valued because it can contain diamonds.

Red and gold

For thousands of years, people have used garnets of all colors in necklaces and rings that show their status and power. And gold is the perfect metal to offset the glow of a red garnet.

ECLOGITE SAMPLES

Eclogite from blocks in kimberlite

Eclogite rock

Mining eclogite

Eclogites rarely come to the surface, so eclogite mines are rare. La Gerbaudière quarry in the Loire valley in France has been mined for the minerals found in eclogite since the 1970s.

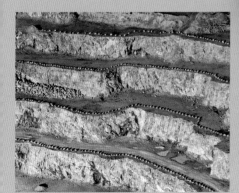

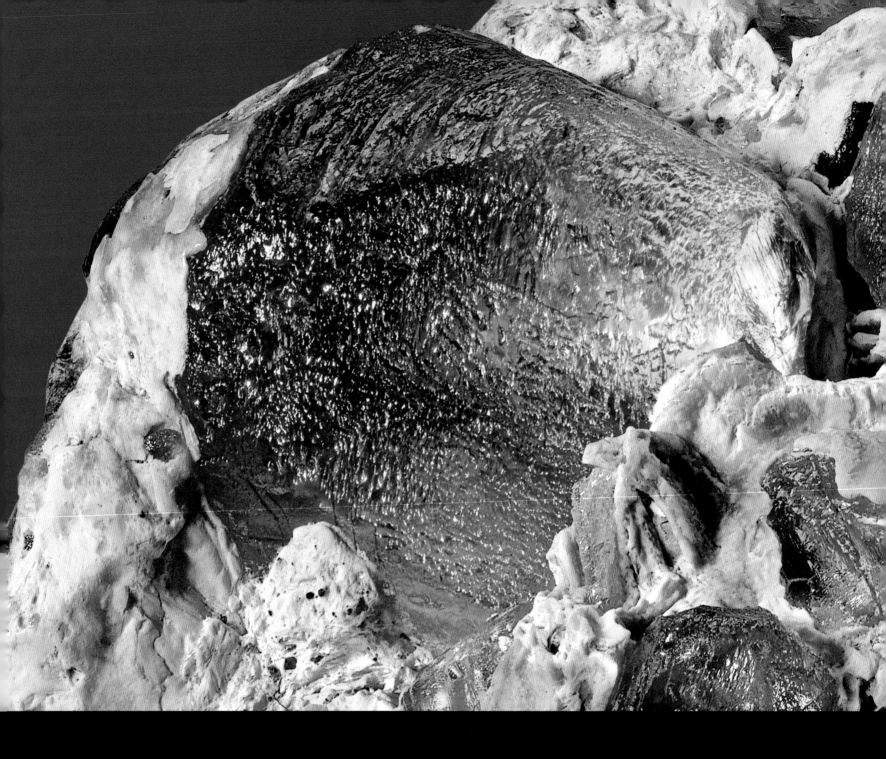

Only 130 out of 5,000 minerals are considered good enough to become gemstones, and of these less than 50 are frequently used. Gems are rare because certain minerals and elements must collect in the right space, and at the right temperature and pressure for long enough to allow them to form.

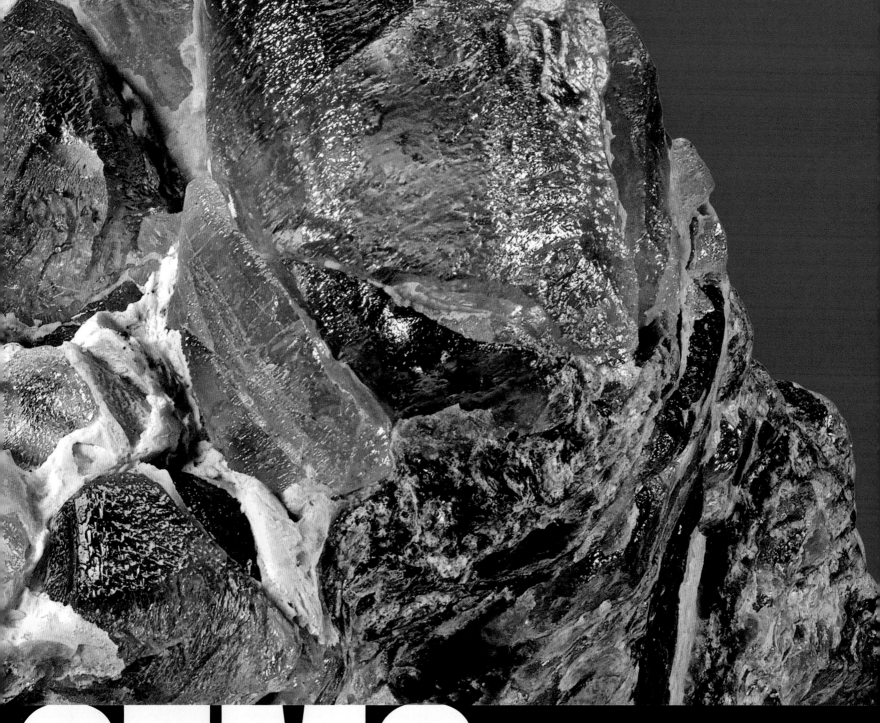

GEMS

GEM GALLERY

Dealers rate gemstones on the four Cs: clarity, color, cut, and carat. A flawless transparent crystal sparkles brilliantly, so it has great clarity, while vivid colors are highly prized. Gemstones must be tough to withstand the cutting that brings out their sparkle and color, and they are weighed in carats.

Jet

Rough
tourmailne

Watermelon
tourmaline

**Rough
diamond**
These are collectors'
items themselves. If it was
cut, this diamond would likely
be worth only a small percentage
more than what it would fetch
if it was simply polished.

Polished
aquamarine
stone

Rose
quartz

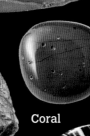

Coral

Diamond

Agate

Labradorite

Sunstone

Tourmaline
with

Rough ruby

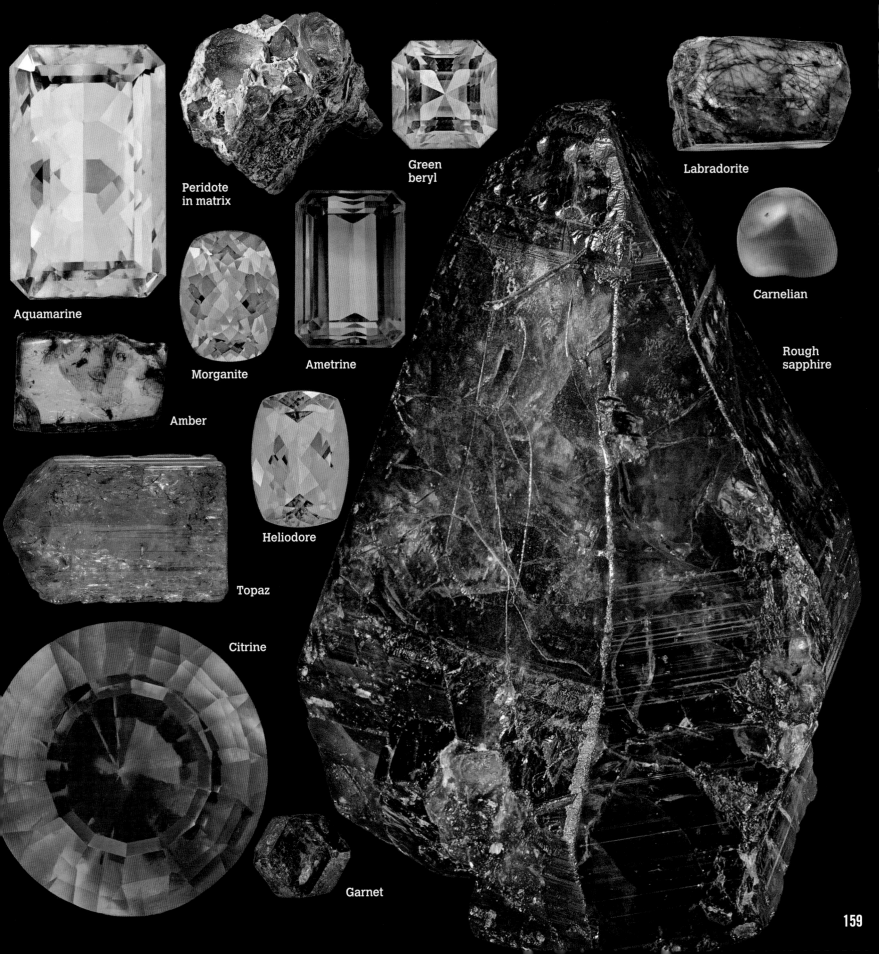

Aquamarine

Peridote
in matrix

Green
beryl

Labradorite

Carnelian

Morganite

Ametrine

Rough
sapphire

Amber

Heliodore

Topaz

Citrine

Garnet

159

GARNET

HARD SILICATE

Garnets can fool us—even with their name, which comes from the Latin word for "pomegranate," with its bright red seeds. But garnets can be many shades of red, brown, or even green or blue. They have been used as gems for thousands of years because they are beautiful and plentiful, and they do not need much polishing to shine.

Garnet Star Nebula
There is a large, dusty nebula in the constellation Cepheus. It is 3,000 light-years away from Earth and is one of the largest nebulae visible from our planet. The bright star at the top is Mu Cephei, or the Garnet Star, which was named by the astronomer William Herschel in 1783. He noted "a very fine deep garnet color" for the star. The nebula was later named after the star.

Group: silicates

Color: red, brown, nearly black, bright green, yellow, blue, colorless

Hardness: 6.5–7.5

Cleavage: none

Fracture: subconchoidal, uneven

Luster: vitreous to resinous

Streak: white

Specific gravity: 3.7–4.3

Transparency: transparent to translucent

Crystal system: cubic

Uses: ornamental jewelry; glass paper for sanding; abrasive powders and granules; water-jet cutting; indicator mineral for mineral exploration; filtration

Garnet
Dark, bloodred garnets like this one are the most sought-after type. There are more than 20 varieties in the garnet group. Of these, there are 6 main types that are used as gems: pyrope, almandite, spessartite, grossularite, andradite, and uvarovite.

Noah's Ark
According to the Talmud, the central text of Judaism, a garnet carbuncle was fixed to the mast of Noah's Ark to provide light day and night. From that time onward, the garnet was considered to be a protection for travelers.

Uncut green garnet

In 1967, a British geologist was looking for gemstones in northeast Tanzania when he came across rocks that held beautiful green fragments. These turned out to be green grossularite. The gem that is cut from this stone is called tsavorite, a name proposed by the then president of Tiffany & Co., in honor of Tsavo National Park in Kenya.

Watch movement

From the early 18th century, natural gems were used as bearings in the mechanical movements of wristwatches. The stones used were mostly garnets, rubies, and sapphires. At the beginning of the 20th century, a method for producing synthetic sapphires was invented, and most jewel bearings today are synthetic sapphires made from hard corundum.

Garnet jewelry

If worn on the body, garnets were said to attract riches, wisdom, honor, and glory. They have been worn as jewelry from the earliest times—a garnet called "the Wise One" was set in the crown of the German emperor Otto (912–973).

GARNET SAMPLES

Orange-brown garnet

Hessonite garnet

Andradite garnet

Grossular garnet

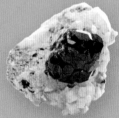

Spessartine garnet in quartz and granite

Rough garnet

BERYL

SILICATE MINERAL

Beryl is harder than quartz so it wears well, and it comes in a sparkling range of colors. White beryl is known as goshenite; pink is called morganite after the famous American banker and gem collector J. P. Morgan; and red beryl is a rare, deep crimson variety. Emerald and aquamarine are also types of beryl.

BERYL SAMPLES

Rough beryl

Rough morganite

Cushion-cut morganite

Rough beryl

Cut red beryl (bixbite)

Group: silicates

Color: pale to bright green, yellow, white

Luster: vitreous

Hardness: 7.5–8

Cleavage: indistinct

Fracture: uneven to conchoidal; brittle

Luster: vitreous

Streak: white

Specific gravity: 2.6–2.8

Crystal system: hexagonal

Uses: jewelry; computers; beryllium alloys; scanning equipment; lasers; airbags; braking systems; tsunami detection; radar; weather satellites

Golden beryl
Golden beryl or heliodor, from the Greek for "gift of the sun," was made famous by a set of jewelry designed for Kaiser Wilhelm II by Lucas von Cranach in 1914.

Green beryl
Only beryl with the deepest green color is called emerald (see pages 166–167). The lighter green stones are simply known as green beryls.

Pink beryl
Morganite, or pink beryl, is a rare stone, first discovered in Pala, CA in the early 20th century. Stones like this are much prized and often placed in settings with diamonds.

The **largest beryl** was found in **Madagascar in 1976**—60 ft (18 m) long and weighing **84,000 pounds (380,000 kg)**.

Rough-cut beryl

This mineral has many varieties and ranges in color from tan to pale green. In addition to the colors shown on the previous page, there is a colorless variety is called goshenite, and a raspberry-red beryl called pezzottaite. The rare, deep red beryl, or bixbite, is found only in Utah.

"BERYLLIUM"

Beryllium was once known as glucinium, from the Greek word for "sweet." But do not go tasting to see if it really is sweet, since this element is highly toxic and will damage your body. Beryllium is very strong and lightweight, with a high melting point.

Elemental

This gray metallic element is extracted from the minerals beryl and bertrandite. Beryllium is very valuable because it is one-third as light as aluminum, and six times stiffer than steel.

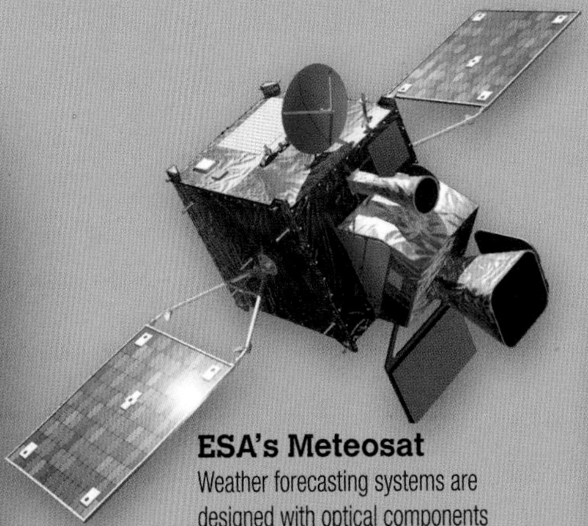

ESA's Meteosat

Weather forecasting systems are designed with optical components made of beryllium. These allow satellites—like this one from the European Space Agency—to predict and track weather patterns.

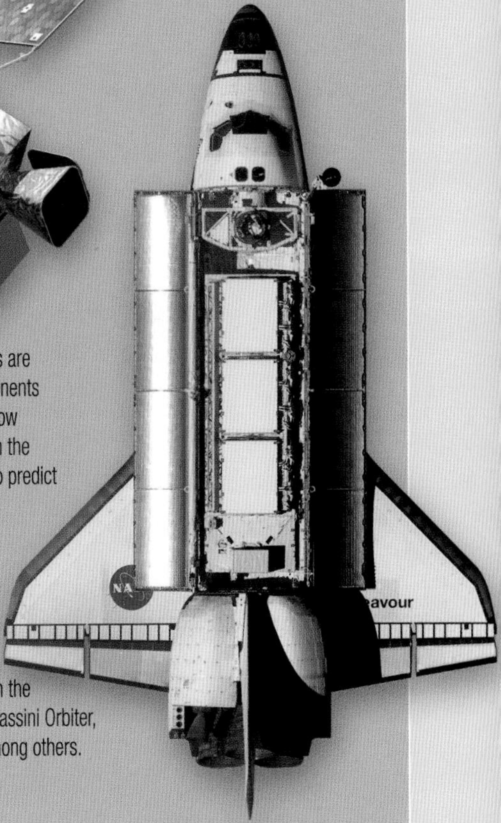

Space shuttle

Since the early days of space flight, beryllium has been valuable because of its strength, light weight, and reflectivity. It was used in the Space Shuttle, the Mars Rover, the Cassini Orbiter, and the Hubble Space Telescope, among others.

Evacuate!

Beryllium plays an essential role in undersea systems that give warnings about earthquakes and tsunamis so that people can evacuate coastal regions in time. The systems are protected by housings made of copper beryllium. This picture shows the devastated town of Sendai, Japan after an earthquake triggered a tsunami in 2011.

EMERALD

SILICATE MINERAL

Deep green emeralds have a beautiful and unusual color—something that has been valued from ancient times right up to the present. Most emeralds contain tiny pieces of other minerals, liquids, or gases, which are known as *jardin*—French for "garden"—maybe because they look like plant roots amid the green.

Group: silicates

Color: deep green

Luster: vitreous

Hardness: 7.5–8

Cleavage: indistinct

Fracture: uneven to conchoidal; brittle

Luster: vitreous

Streak: white

Specific gravity: 2.6–3.0

Crystal system: hexagonal

Uses: jewelry

EMERALD SAMPLES

Rough emeralds in matrix

Prismatic emerald crystal

Bright green emerald rods in matrix

Cleopatra

The earliest known emerald mine was in the valley of Wadi Sikait in Egypt's eastern desert, and it operated from the 1st century BCE. It is said that one of the most fabulous emerald collections was that of Queen Cleopatra (69–30 BCE). It is quite possible, however, that many of the stones that Cleopatra wore were actually peridots (see page 41).

In **2011,** an emerald necklace owned by the actress **Elizabeth Taylor** sold for **$6.5 million.**

arest of the rare

...eralds without imperfections are extremely rare,
...they can be worth more than diamonds. A stepped
..., called an emerald cut—usually rectangular,
...re octagonal—was devised so that a minimum
...material would be lost in the process. Emerald cuts
...e often used for diamonds (see pages 196–197).

Emerald lore

According to Indian mythology, the name emerald comes from Sanskrit and means "the green of growing things." It was believed to prevent epilepsy and cure dysentery, and it is said that if you put an emerald under your tongue, you will see the future.

Shipwreck treasure

In the 16th century, Conquistadors discovered the emeralds that the South American Inca and Aztec nations had prized for so long. The Spanish began a trade in emeralds across Europe and Asia. This emerald brooch was recovered from a Spanish ship, *Las Maravillas*, that sank in the Bahamas in 1656.

Emerald in the rough

Emerald crystals are often found as long, hexagonal prisms with flat ends. Although they are hard, they often have flaws and surface-reaching fractures that make them difficult to cut.

Quetzal

The Aztec name for emeralds was *quetzalitzli* because their color was so like the green feathers of the quetzal. This bird was a symbol of seasonal renewal for them.

Synthetic emeralds

Synthetic gem crystals have been made since the late 1800s, often for industrial use. Today, many lab-grown emeralds are virtually indistinguishable from the real gem, so there are very strict rules about how they are sold.

Green buddha

Many objects are misnamed and the Emerald Buddha is no exception. Despite its name, it is carved from jade (see pages 202–203).

Gem of a find

In 1998, field geologist Bill Wengzynowski made an exciting discovery at Regal Ridge in Yukon: Canada's first emerald deposit. This was only one of several veins that were found, most surrounded by overlapping masses of fine, dark tourmaline crystals. There were green beryl crystals up to 1.5 inches (4 cm) in length; some of the smaller crystals and sections of larger crystals were gem quality, including the raw emeralds pictured here. Although at first the emeralds appeared dull brown, they have green flecks and fluoresce in sunlight.

AQUAMARINE
SILICATE MINERAL

Rough aquamarine

Rough aquamarine

Aquamarine crystal on albite

Aquamarine crystals in matrix

Large aquamarine in matrix

The bluish green of this stone gives it its name, from the Latin words for "water" and "sea." Both emeralds and aquamarines are part of the beryl family, but unlike emeralds, aquamarines are usually completely flawless, so they have a glasslike quality.

Group: silicates

Color: clear, blue, greenish blue, blue-green

Hardness: 7.5–8

Cleavage: indistinct

Fracture: uneven to conchoidal; brittle

Luster: vitreous

Streak: white

Specific gravity: 2.6–2.8

Transparency: transparent to translucent

Crystal system: hexagonal

Uses: ornamental jewelry

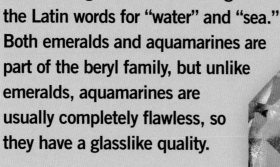

All at sea
Aquamarine was said to protect sailors and bring them safely home. The Romans thought that the stone was sacred to Neptune, the god of the sea. They said that he found the stone when it fell out of a jewel box belonging to the Sirens, fabulous creatures whose singing lured sailors to their doom on the rocks.

Worth its weight
Aquamarine can be blue, greenish blue, or blue-green. The most valuable color is a dark blue. Most of the aquamarine that is sold today has been heat-treated to make it a purer blue. Precious gemstones are weighed in carats (ct). This aquamarine octagon is 56.88 carats—in other words, it weighs 0.40 ounces (11.34 g).

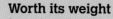

The largest **cut aquamarine**—cut from the **Minas Gerais** mine, Brazil, in 1980—weighs nearly **5 pounds (2.3 kg)**.

Rough aquamarine
Huge crystals of aquamarine are produced when the cooling rate of the rock has been slow. The color comes from trace amounts of iron that become embedded in the colorless and transparent beryl crystals.

Crystal lens
It is said that the Roman emperor Nero wore a monocle made of aquamarine. The German word for "eyeglasses" is *brille*, which comes from the word *beryl*. When the Germans first began to make eyeglasses, they used slivers of aquamarine as lenses to correct shortsightedness.

Crystals in rock
Aquamarine crystals are often found as perfect individual six-sided hexagons. However, they also develop in groups as short, stubby crystals. They are also frequently found with topaz (see pages 188–189).

Magnificent pendant
This magnificent pendant with its aquamarines, sapphires, pearls, and gold dates from 1867. It was made in England during the "Grand Period" of Victorian jewelry, when items reflected the opulence of the time, with industry flourishing and millionaires being created overnight.

TOURMALINE

BOROSILICATE MINERAL

Elvis and Dr. Nick
Elvis gave this ring—cat's-eye green tourmaline and diamond mounted in 14-karat yellow gold—to his friend and physician George C. Nichopoulos after a concert because it matched his shirt. The two men were known as "the King and Dr. Nick."

TOURMALINE SAMPLES

Rough watermelon tourmaline

Cut watermelon tourmaline

Dravite tourmaline

Green tourmaline crystals

Black tourmaline crystal

Tourmaline is a mongrel gem—it does not come from just one mineral, but from a group that includes elbaite, schorl, and dravite. This tough gem is often found in rivers after its parent rock has weathered away—and it comes in more colors than any other gemstone. The word *tourmaline* is from the Sri Lankan words for "multicolored stone."

Group:	silicates
Color:	black, brown; sometimes gray, yellow, blue, green, red, pink, colorless, white; may be zoned
Hardness:	7–7.5
Cleavage:	indistinct
Fracture:	uneven to conchoidal; brittle
Luster:	vitreous to resinous
Streak:	white
Specific gravity:	2.9–3.2
Transparency:	transparent to opaque
Crystal system:	trigonal, hexagonal
Uses:	ornamental jewelry; figurines; high-pressure gauges

Polished yellow tourmaline
This pale yellow tourmaline is faceted in a round brilliant cut. The colors of this canary tourmaline happen because the mineral is rich in manganese, with traces of titanium. The most valuable gems are the brightest yellow.

Rainbow rock
The ancient Egyptians called tourmaline "rainbow rock," since they thought that it gathered up all the colors of the rainbow as it traveled up through Earth. They had a point, because tourmaline comes in more colors than any other gemstone.

Tourmaline sunangel

This tiny hummingbird—only 4 inches (10 cm) in length—lives in the forests of Colombia and Ecuador. Its name is clearly prompted by the dominant glittering green feathers, offset by the other white, black, and bronze plumage.

Pyroelectricity

An electrical potential is created in tourmaline when it is heated. The heat changes the positions of some of the atoms in the crystal, causing a voltage surge. This was first written about by the German Franz Aepinus in 1759, in his *Theory of Electricity and Magnetism*.

Cixi

The empress dowager Cixi (1835–1908), of the Manchu Yehenara clan, unofficially controlled the Qing dynasty in China for 47 years. Most of the pink and red tourmaline mined in California was shipped to China because the empress was particularly fond of the colors. Chinese artisans carved the gems into snuffboxes and jewelry.

Rough cut

These magnificent crystals of multicolored tourmaline are embedded with clevelandite, a white variety of feldspar. Tourmaline is often found in pegmatite dikes in granite but is also common in gneiss, schist, limestone, and dolomite.

171

Gem-quality tourmaline

These long green tourmaline crystals are embedded in quartz. Tourmaline is found in granites—especially where altered by hot fluids—pegmatites, and sometimes in adjacent rocks. Today, major gem specimens are mined in Brazil and Africa. In the United States, the gem was first discovered in October 1821 by two hikers, Elijah Hamlin and Ezekiel Holmes. Later, Hamlin's younger brothers, Cyrus and Hannibal (who later served as vice president to Abraham Lincoln), found more green and red tourmaline near the original site.

AGATE

BANDED CHALCEDONY

Bands form in agate as minerals and other impurities seep into the water-filled cavities inside igneous rocks. The result is a huge range of colors forming interesting patterns across the gem—so pleasing to us that agates were some of the first stones made into jewelry, 20,000 years ago.

AGATE SAMPLES

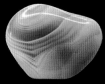

Chalcedony crystal

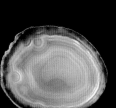

Section of orange agate

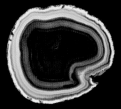

Section of green-and-brown agate

Blue lace agate

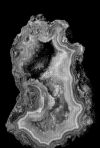

Agate geode crystal growth

Group: silicates

Color: colorless, white, yellow, gray, brown, blue, red; banded

Hardness: 6.5–7

Cleavage: none

Fracture: conchoidal

Luster: waxy to vitreous

Streak: white

Specific gravity: 2.4–2.7

Transparency: translucent to opaque

Crystal system: hexagonal, trigonal

Uses: ornaments; jewelry; cameos; animal carvings; bookends; statues; figurines

Agate geode
This cut and polished agate geode shows just how stunning the color combinations of these stones can be. On the outside, geodes appear to be nothing but dull brown rock. Look into the interior, and there is a treasure-house of multicolored crystals.

Agate Bridge, Arizona
Over the centuries, floodwaters have washed away the sandstone around and below this agate log so that it now forms a bridge above a gully. Some 225 million years ago, tall trees washed into this area and were buried beneath a mixture of mud, silt, and volcanic ashes. Silica deposits replaced the wood and crystallized into quartz.

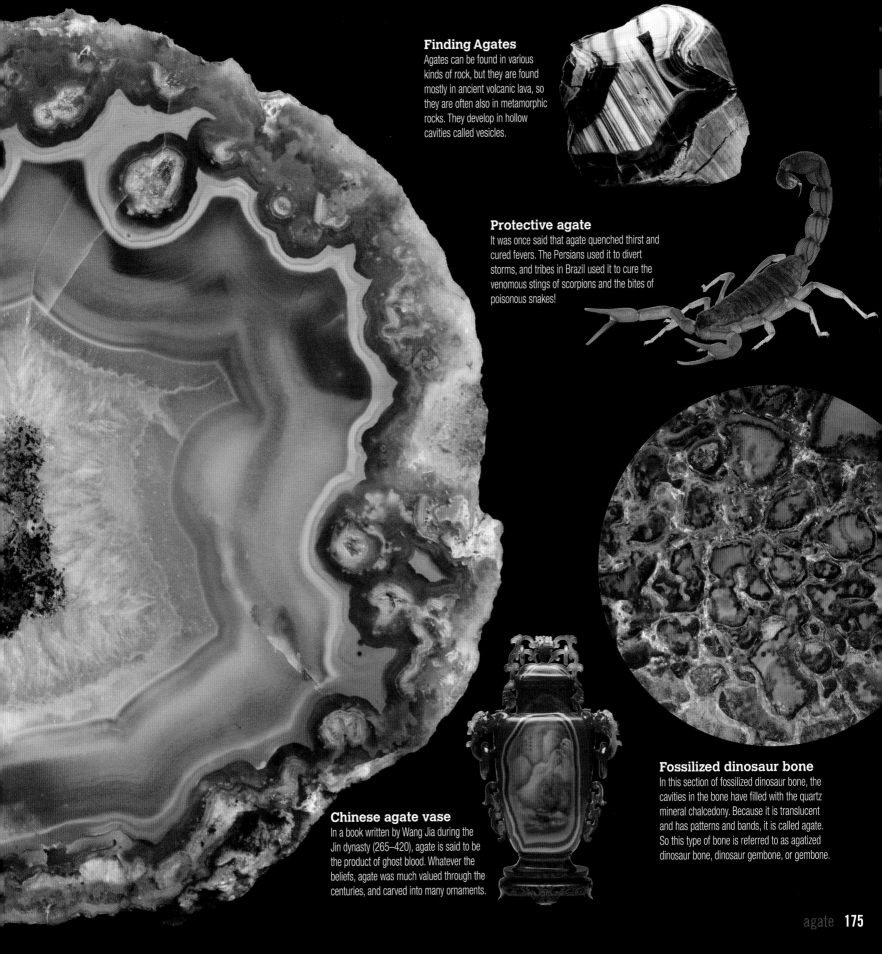

Finding Agates

Agates can be found in various kinds of rock, but they are found mostly in ancient volcanic lava, so they are often also in metamorphic rocks. They develop in hollow cavities called vesicles.

Protective agate

It was once said that agate quenched thirst and cured fevers. The Persians used it to divert storms, and tribes in Brazil used it to cure the venomous stings of scorpions and the bites of poisonous snakes!

Chinese agate vase

In a book written by Wang Jia during the Jin dynasty (265–420), agate is said to be the product of ghost blood. Whatever the beliefs, agate was much valued through the centuries, and carved into many ornaments.

Fossilized dinosaur bone

In this section of fossilized dinosaur bone, the cavities in the bone have filled with the quartz mineral chalcedony. Because it is translucent and has patterns and bands, it is called agate. So this type of bone is referred to as agatized dinosaur bone, dinosaur gembone, or gembone.

QUARTZ

SILICON DIOXIDE

QUARTZ SAMPLES

Aventurine stone

Carnelian in matrix

Heliotrope, or bloodstone

Amethyst crystals

Eisenkiesel quartz

Take one part silicon and two parts oxygen— that is the recipe for quartz, the most common mineral on our planet. In its colorless form, it is called rock crystal (see page 128), but when impurities seep in, they bring with them new colors. This is how purple amethyst, yellow citrine, and smoky brown quartz are formed.

Group: silicates

Color: all colors, from black or purple to red or green to yellow, white, or colorless

Hardness: 7

Cleavage: none

Fracture: conchoidal

Luster: vitreous

Streak: white

Specific gravity: 2.6

Transparency: transparent to translucent

Crystal system: hexagonal, trigonal

Uses: carvings; jewelry; construction industry; oscillators; quartz crystals in accurate timepieces; glass manufacturing; sandblasting; silicon semiconductors

Rose quartz
This rosy pink variety of quartz is found all over the world and can occur in large quantities. However, it is often not very transparent, so it is not as popular as the pink varieties of other gems, such as topaz and tourmaline.

The Alfred Jewel
Inscribed with the words *Aelfred mec heht gewyrcan*— "Alfred ordered me to be made"—the Alfred Jewel is made of enamel and quartz enclosed in gold. It refers to Alfred the Great of Britain, who died in 899. The jewel was found in 1693 when it was plowed up in a field in Somerset.

Close to **70 percent** of all **sand grains** on Earth **are made of quartz**, formed by weathering.

QUARTZ MYTHS AND LEGENDS

Many stones have attracted people's attention over the centuries, whether as potential jewelry or for use as talismans or in medicine. Myths and legends have grown around them—some that reflect the stones' appearances or properties, but also some that are, quite simply, bizarre!

Chalcedony
This cryptocrystalline quartz was sacred to Diana, Roman goddess of the hunt. It was worn or placed on the altar when performing rituals in her honor. Romans also believed that it brought victory in arguments.

Tigereye
This stone was believed to be all-seeing. Roman soldiers wore it into battle to deflect weapons and to give them courage. It was also thought to give them insight into the battle situation.

Green jasper
In a poem called the *Lithica*, written in the 4th century, the author claimed that wearing green jasper would bring rain to parched lands. It was also thought to drive away evil spirits.

Smoky quartz
Smoky quartz was known as the "stone of power" and was often used as a divination stone. It was used to dissolve pain and regulate the body's functions. Smoky quartz and rock crystal were both used to make crystal balls used by Gypsy fortune-tellers.

Rock crystal
Pure quartz is called rock crystal. It is colorless and has no flaws. It is transparent or translucent and often used for imitation diamonds, although it lacks fire.

Rose quartz
This "love stone" has the power to heal a broken heart. It is the stone of love, warmth, and compassion.

Quartz in all its glory

Quartz is the most abundant individual mineral in Earth's crust, and one of the most varied in form and color. There are many different types of quartz, some of them imaginatively named. For example, phantom quartz contains ghostlike layers within a crystal, while cactus quartz has large crystals overgrown with a layer of spiky smaller crystals. Star quartz, when polished, displays a six-rayed star (this is known as an asterism), and Herkimer diamonds are exceptionally clear quartzes from the Mohawk Valley region of central New York State.

AMETHYST

VITREOUS QUARTZ

Amethyst
crystal

Amethyst
crystals

Section of
amethyst geode

Amethyst
geode

Section of
amethyst geode

In ancient Rome, senators, victorious generals, and emperors wore purple on their togas, as have many kings and queens in later centuries. This is because the color is linked with high status—which also explains why the amethyst has been called the "jewel of the gods," and why people wear jewelry decorated with this beautiful gem.

Group: silicate

Color: almost white to deep violet, mauve, and purple; also pale red-violet

Hardness: 7

Cleavage: none

Fracture: conchoidal

Luster: vitreous

Streak: white

Specific gravity: 2.7

Transparency: transparent to opaque

Crystal system: hexagonal, trigonal

Uses: jewelry; ornaments; cabochons; collectors' items

Dionysus
In Greek legend, Dionysus, the god of wine, was angry and swore revenge on the first person who crossed his path. He created two fierce tigers. An innocent young girl named Amethystos was passing; to save her, the goddess Artemis changed her into a statue of pure crystal. Dionysus was mortified and wept tears of wine, which colored the stone purple.

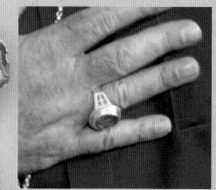

Bishop's ring
The color purple has been used from ancient times to symbolize a person of status or a leader. A bishop wears purple robes and a ring that normally contains an amethyst. People kiss the ring as a mark of respect for this representative of the church.

Cut amethyst
Because the color distribution in amethyst crystals varies, the gems are often cut as brilliant rounds or ovals (right) to maximize the color. Lower-grade amethysts may have their color enhanced by being heated. The stones are in demand for designer pieces and mass-market jewelry alike.

Amethyst geode
Growing in pyramid-shaped crystals, amethysts get their color from iron and manganese impurities. They are usually transparent, but some translucent to opaque amethyst is also found; the purple areas alternate with white or gray zones.

The world's **largest amethyst** geode is the **Empress of Uruguay,** which is **10.7 feet (3.3 m)** tall.

Leonardo da Vinci
During the Renaissance, amethyst was considered to be a symbol of humility and modesty. The great artist and inventor Leonardo da Vinci (1452–1519) said that "amethyst dissipates evil thoughts and quickens the intelligence." He also believed that the power of meditation increased ten times when done in purple light.

The world's **largest** faceted citrine, the **Malaga**, weighs **20,200 carats** (8.8 pounds, or 4 kg).

Ametrine

This beautiful cut octagon is a unique mixture of amethyst and citrine. It is also known as bolivianite, since all naturally occurring ametrine is mined from the Anahí mine in southeastern Bolivia, in South America. It is said that, in the 1500s, the mine was given to a Spanish conquistador named Don Felipe as dowry for his marriage to Princess Anahí of the Ayoreo tribe. When Felipe had to flee the country, Anahi was fatally injured but gave him an ametrine as a symbol of her undying love.

CITRINE SAMPLES

Tumbled
citrine quartz

Citrine crystal

Rough citrine

Section of
citrine geode

Section of
citrine geode

Yellow jewel

Citrine is a popular jewel, often worn in pendants. It is easily confused with other yellow gems such as topaz (see pages 188–189) and yellow sapphire (see pages 192–193). Citrine is much softer than either topaz or sapphire.

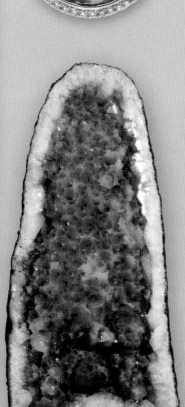

CITRINE

SILICON DIOXIDE

Citrine is named for *citrum*, the Latin word for "lemon," because of its yellow color, which is caused by trace quantities of iron impurities. It occurs very rarely, so citrine is the most valued quartz gem. Most of today's citrine is made artificially by heat treatment because so few citrines are golden.

Group: silicates

Color: yellow, yellow-brown, golden, dark amber

Hardness: 7

Cleavage: none

Fracture: conchoidal

Luster: vitreous

Streak: colorless

Specific gravity: 2.7

Transparency: transparent to nearly opaque

Crystal system: hexagonal, trigonal

Uses: jewelry; ornaments; cabochons; collectors' items

Citrine wagtail

This bird is aptly named, since the male citrine wagtail in his summer plumage has a bright yellow head and underparts.

Natural citrine

Citrine is found all over the world in igneous and metamorphic rocks, particularly in granite and gneiss. It is often found alongside amethyst, but it is much rarer than its purple cousin. The crystals are typically found in geodes and are usually small in size.

Heat treatment

Much of the commercial citrine on the market is heat-treated, which enhances its color so that it takes on a deep orange or slightly reddish tint.

Smoky citrine quartz

The yellow color of smoky citrine is created by the amount of aluminum and lithium in the stone. The ratio of the two elements to each other determines whether the crystal turns smoky or citrine when it is exposed to irradiation. Natural smoky citrine is rare.

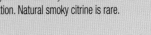

OPAL

HYDRATED SILICA

Opal is a very unusual gem, because the silica inside is shaped into tiny spheres, not the usual crystals. The spheres scatter light to produce many different colors—this is called opalescence—and can even change color when heated. They also explain why this gem cracks and chips easily.

OPAL SAMPLES

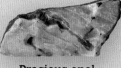

Precious opal with yellow potch

Honey opal

Rough opal in matrix

Polished fire opal

Opal in matrix

Group: silicates

Color: white, yellow, red, brown, blue, green, black; usually pale

Hardness: 5.5–6.5

Cleavage: none

Fracture: conchoidal

Luster: vitreous

Streak: white

Specific gravity: 1.8–2.3

Transparency: transparent to translucent

Crystal system: amorphous

Uses: jewelry; ornaments; cabochons; abrasives; insulation; fillers; ceramics

Rough opal

Opal is considered to be a mineraloid, rather than a mineral, because it does not have a crystalline structure or definite chemical compostion. It is formed from a solution of silicon dioxide and water.

Potch opals

Common opals are called potch opals and are white, honey colored, red, or black. About 95 percent of all opal mined is potch. Although they do not exhibit the play of color of precious opals, they have commercial value and are also cut and polished as gemstones.

Mining the opal fields

Australia's opal fields lie in the three states of Queensland, New South Wales, and South Australia, along the site of an ancient great inland sea. This mine is at Coober Pedy in South Australia, which is considered the opal capital of the world. The gems are mined from sedimentary rocks such as sandstone and ironstone; some opals are found only 8 inches (20 cm) below ground.

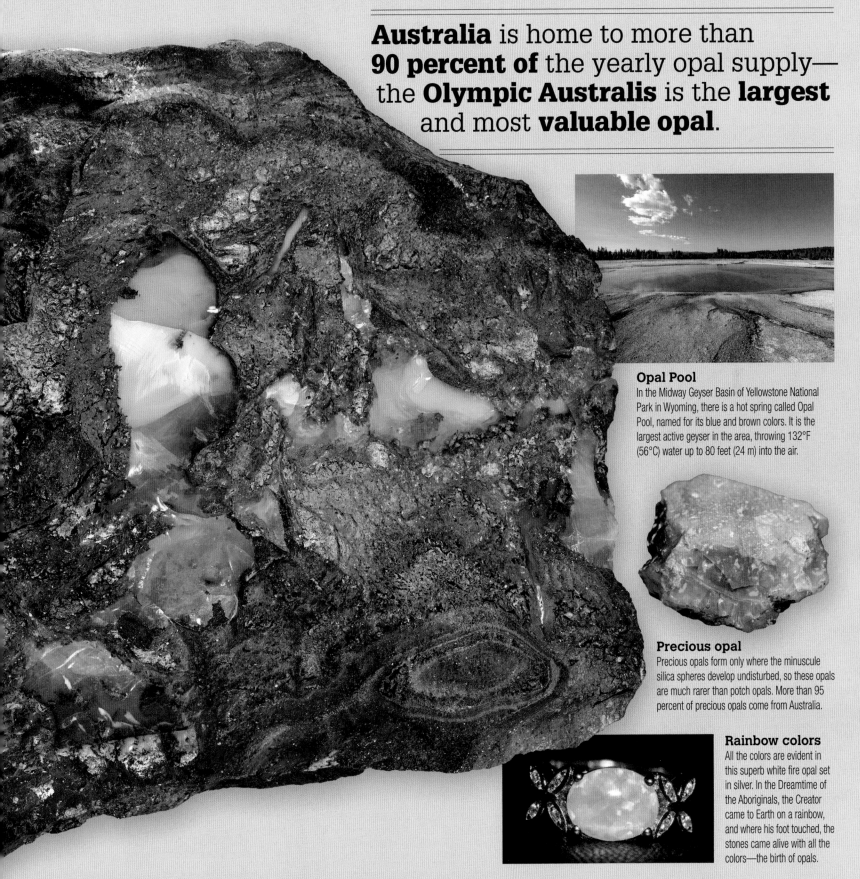

Australia is home to more than 90 percent of the yearly opal supply— the Olympic Australis is the largest and most valuable opal.

Opal Pool
In the Midway Geyser Basin of Yellowstone National Park in Wyoming, there is a hot spring called Opal Pool, named for its blue and brown colors. It is the largest active geyser in the area, throwing 132°F (56°C) water up to 80 feet (24 m) into the air.

Precious opal
Precious opals form only where the minuscule silica spheres develop undisturbed, so these opals are much rarer than potch opals. More than 95 percent of precious opals come from Australia.

Rainbow colors
All the colors are evident in this superb white fire opal set in silver. In the Dreamtime of the Aboriginals, the Creator came to Earth on a rainbow, and where his foot touched, the stones came alive with all the colors—the birth of opals.

Precious stone

The opal is Australia's national gemstone for good reason: More than 90 percent of the world's supply of this glorious gem is produced there. Australian opal resulted from a unique circumstance. Between 100 and 97 million years ago, the Eromanga Sea that covered 60 percent of the continent started to retreat. The central Australian landscape began to dry out, and an acidic weathering took place, releasing silica. The acidity then lowered to a level at which opal could form. Similar conditions have been observed on the surface of Mars.

TOPAZ

SILICATE MINERAL

Topaz has confused people for centuries. Until about 200 years ago, all yellow gems were called topaz, when in fact some were quartz, beryl, olivine, or sapphire. And not all topaz is yellow: It can be all sorts of colors, from yellow to blue or violet. A lot of modern topaz is artificially colored.

TOPAZ SAMPLES

Topaz on quartz

Cut blue oval topaz

Rough brown topaz

Rough blue topaz

Topaz crystal

Group: silicates

Color: colorless, straw yellow, pale blue, pale green, pink, brown

Hardness: 8

Cleavage: perfect, basal

Fracture: subconchoidal to uneven

Luster: vitreous

Streak: none

Specific gravity: 3.4–3.6

Transparency: transparent to translucent

Crystal system: orthorhombic

Uses: jewelry; cabochons; abrasives; knife sharpeners; grinding equipment

Topaz gems

The size of gems can vary enormously. This square-cut orange topaz is 6.10 carats (0.04 ounces, or 1.22 g). The American Golden Topaz is the largest cut yellow topaz, and one of the largest faceted gems in the world, with 172 facets. It weighs in at an amazing 22,892.50 carats (10.09 pounds, or 4.58 kg).

Topaz minerals

Topaz is found in mountainous areas around the world. The crystals grow in fractures and cavities of igneous rocks such as granite, rhyolite, and pegmatite. The largest crystals are found in Brazil, and blue topaz is mined in the Ural Mountains of Russia.

Color of the Sun

Some scholars link the origin of *topaz* with the Sanskrit *tapaz*, meaning "fire," "burn," or "hot." Ancient Egyptians believed that the topaz was colored with the golden glow of the sun god Re.

Alchemist's stone

Medieval alchemists believed that if they found the mysterious philosopher's stone, they would be able to turn base materials into gold, restore youth, and even create life. This alchemist is attempting to create life with the flash of fire from a topaz crystal.

In 1944, it was reported that a 385-ton topaz crystal had been found in Brazil.

Imperial topaz

The most sought-after and rarest natural topaz is imperial topaz, also known as precious topaz. This stunning crystal is found in peach, pink, or orange colors and was named in honor of 17th-century Russian czars, who claimed the exclusive rights to the mining of the gemstones in the Ural Mountains.

Treated topaz

Most modern topaz is colored artificially with heat and coatings of metallic oxides. In most cases, the added color is confined to the surface of the gemstone. The coating can wear thin over time.

MORE GEMS

The biggest and most famous gems have great stories to tell, because they have been coveted, worn, fought over, and stolen by royalty and the rich. The stories of their lives after they were cut and polished can be as exciting as the sagas of how they were born.

Cut sapphire

Blue topaz

Orange topaz

Garnet

Rough topaz on quartz

Most gemstones look dull when they are mined. Early gemstones were rubbed together to make their surfaces smooth. Now they are cut and polished. Sometimes they are mixed with grit and water and tumbled in a machine to make them smooth and round.

Polished opal

Opal

Peach
sapphire

Yellow diamond

Rough
sapphire

Polished
opal

Ruby

Rose quartz

Smoky
quartz

Tiger's
eye

Rhodochrosite

Lapis
lazuli

Emerald

Smoky
quartz

Turquoise

Polished
lapis
lazuli

SAPPHIRE

BLUE CORUNDUM

Sapphire is one of the few blue gems. Tiny amounts of iron and titanium added to corundum create a color that led ancient Persians to believe that Earth rested on a giant sapphire whose reflection colored the sky. To add to its star appeal, tiny amounts of the mineral rutile can make light reflect like a six-rayed star.

Blue sapphire

Sapphire sounds much more exotic than *blue corundum*, which is what it is. Traces of iron and titanium create the depth of color. This gem can also be pink, yellow, or green, as well as many other colors; such stones are called "fancy" sapphires.

SAPPHIRE SAMPLES

Oval peach sapphire

Rough sapphire

Sapphire crystal

Rough blue sapphire

Rough, dark blue sapphire

Group: oxides

Color: colorless, yellow, blue, violet, pink, red-orange, brown, green, purple

Hardness: 9

Cleavage: none

Fracture: conchoidal to uneven

Luster: adamantine to vitreous

Streak: colorless

Specific gravity: 4.0–4.1

Transparency: transparent to translucent

Crystal system: hexagonal, trigonal

Uses: ornamental jewelry; timepieces; scientific instruments; semiconducting and integrated circuits; sapphire glass for windows

Golden-tailed sapphire

This little hummingbird lives in the forests of South America as well as on the islands of Trinidad and Tobago. It is named for the brilliant iridescent blue of its head and chest. And it is not the only South American bird named after the beautiful blue gemstone. There are several others, including the sapphire quail dove and the sapphire-vented puff-leg.

SAPPHIRES AND ROYALTY

Sapphires, particularly blue sapphires, shine in the crown jewels of many royal families. For centuries, the gem has been linked with the ideas of wisdom and divine favor—very important symbolic connections for any member of a ruling family. So wearing sapphires showed power and strength, but also kindness and sound judgment.

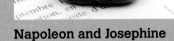

Napoleon and Josephine

On March 24, 2013, the ring that Napoleon gave to his future wife, Josephine, when they were engaged in 1796 was sold for $949,000. It was described by the auction house as a "simple" band decorated with two pear-shaped gems, a blue sapphire and a diamond. Napoleon was young and had very little money at the time.

Saint Wenceslas's crown

The Crown of Saint Wenceslas is one of the crown jewels of Bohemia (now the Czech Republic). Made in 1347 for the coronation of Charles IV, it is wrought of pure gold and decorated with a total of 19 sapphires, 44 spinels, 1 ruby, 30 emeralds, and 20 pearls.

Royal crown of Serbia

The House of Karadjordjevic Crown is one of the crown jewels created in 1904 for the coronation of King Peter I of Serbia (reigned 1903–1921). The crown was made of bronze and set with jewels by the Falize brothers of Paris. They completed the work in three months for 19,000 francs, and were awarded the Serbian Order of St. Sava.

A ring for two princesses

In 2010, Prince William, heir to the throne of England, proposed to Kate Middleton while they were on a romantic holiday in Kenya. In 1981, his mother, Princess Diana, had chosen a blue sapphire ring for her engagement to Prince Charles, and it was this ring that in turn became William and Kate's engagement ring. It is a 12-carat oval blue Ceylon sapphire, surrounded by 14 solitaire diamonds and set in 18-karat gold.

RUBY

RED CORUNDUM

What connects pigeons and diamonds? The ruby. This gem is so rare that a large one can be worth more than a diamond of similar size—the only thing tough enough to cut it. Rubies can vary in shade from almost pink to nearly purple; the most highly prized deep red color is known as pigeon's blood.

Group: oxides

Color: red

Hardness: 9

Cleavage: none

Fracture: conchoidal to uneven

Luster: adamantine to vitreous

Streak: colorless

Specific gravity: 4.0–4.1

Transparency: transparent to translucent

Crystal system: hexagonal, trigonal

Uses: ornamental jewelry; ruby lasers; abrasives; timepieces

Ruby crystals in matrix

Ruby crystal in feldspar

Large ruby crystal

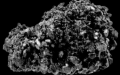

Rough ruby crystals

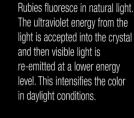

Ruby crystal

Rubies fluoresce in natural light. The ultraviolet energy from the light is accepted into the crystal and then visible light is re-emitted at a lower energy level. This intensifies the color in daylight conditions.

Marco Polo and Kublai Khan

According to an account given by the Italian explorer Marco Polo (1254–1324), the Mongolian emperor Kublai Khan offered the king of Ceylon (today's Sri Lanka) a city in exchange for a ruby the size of his fist. The king answered that he had received the ruby from his ancestors and would pass it on to his descendants.

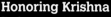

Keepsakes

Rubies have been crafted into impressive jewelry throughout the centuries. In the 19th century, brooches, like this ruby and diamond one, were fashioned as keepsakes or as mourning jewelry.

Honoring Krishna

The Sanskrit word for "ruby" is *ratnaraj*, or "king of precious stones." In Hindu legend, when the demon Vala was destroyed by angry gods, his blood became all the rubies in the world. Ancient Hindus believed that by making an offer of a ruby to the god Krishna, they would be offered rebirth as emperors.

Oval ruby

The ruby's name comes from the Latin *ruber*, meaning "red." This is the second-hardest gemstone after the diamond, and it can be a challenge to cut. Hexagonal, oval, and cushion are the most common shapes.

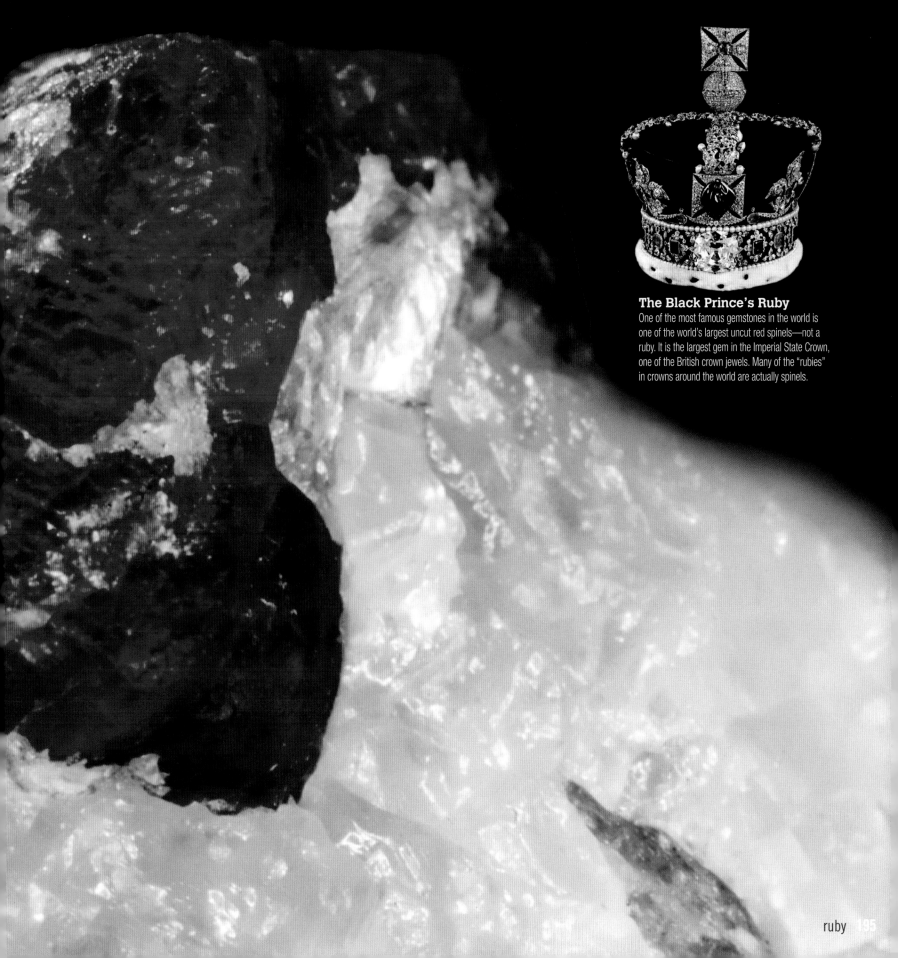

The Black Prince's Ruby

One of the most famous gemstones in the world is one of the world's largest uncut red spinels—not a ruby. It is the largest gem in the Imperial State Crown, one of the British crown jewels. Many of the "rubies" in crowns around the world are actually spinels.

DIAMOND

PURE CARBON

Most diamonds are at least a billion years old, and some may be three times that. Created 100 miles (160 km) down, under incredible heat and pressure, and dragged up by erupting volcanoes, diamonds are extraordinary. They dazzle as jewels, sparkling like no other gem, yet are so tough that only other diamonds can make any impression on them.

DIAMOND SAMPLES

Rough diamond in matrix

Rough uncut diamond

Nikolai Leskov Diamond

Industrial diamond

Group:	native elements
Color:	colorless, white, yellow, red, pink, red, blue, brown, black
Hardness:	10
Cleavage:	perfect
Fracture:	conchoidal
Luster:	adamantine
Streak:	white
Specific gravity:	3.5
Transparency:	transparent to opaque
Crystal system:	cubic
Uses:	jewelry; grinding wheels; drill bits; saw blades; abrasives; speaker domes

Diamond eyes
Many statues of gods and goddesses in India have diamonds for eyes, so that they can see Hindu worshippers clearly. Diamonds are also very important in India for other reasons—nine-tenths of the world's natural diamonds are cut and polished in the Indian state of Gujarat.

Brilliant-cut diamond
Once polished, diamonds reflect light in a way that no other stone does. A brilliant-cut diamond, like this one, is cut with numerous facets so that it reflects life with exceptional brilliance.

Hope Diamond
This legendary blue diamond has had a checkered history, disappearing from view several times. Probably from Golconda, India, its many owners included Louis XIV of France, who bought it in 1668; George IV of England; Henry Philip Hope (from whom it takes its name); and Pierre Cartier, who acquired it in 1909. It is 45.52 carats (0.32 ounces, or 9.10 g) and is now in the Smithsonian Institution's National Museum of Natural History.

55 Cancri e
The Greeks and Romans believed that diamonds were the tears cried by the gods, or splinters from falling stars. And they may not have been far wrong. It is possible that there is a diamond planet out there in space. In 2005, astronomers discovered a planet orbiting the star 55 Cancri. They called the planet 55 Cancri e, and it appears to be made mostly of diamond—theoretically valued at $26.9 nonillion.

The **world's largest** cut diamond is the colorless **Great Star of Africa**, cut from the **Cullinan Diamond**.

Slate mining
Diamond is the hardest natural substance that we know of, and it is chemically resistant. These two qualities make diamonds very suitable as cutting tools in various industries. They are used as drill bits when drilling for oil. Small grains of diamond are embedded in the metal, and they bite through the rock. Here, a diamond saw is being operated in a slate mine.

Diamond crystal

Diamonds are sometimes found in areas where there has been volcanic activity or erosion, or where streams and rivers have carried them. Most diamonds, however, are mined from blue igneous rocks called kimberlites. These are created deep inside Earth at very high temperatures and under enormous pressure. Kimberlite magma is carried to the surface by volcanic eruptions; while traveling upward, it acquires xenoliths, or "foreign rocks." Diamonds are among these xenoliths. Most diamonds formed 1 to 3.6 billion years ago.

TURQUOISE

HYDRATED COPPER

The ancient peoples of Africa, Asia, and South and North America all used turquoise as gems and for decoration. This shows the amazing allure of its blue-green color, and how easy it is to shape, being relatively soft. In turn it has given its name to a popular color.

TURQUOISE SAMPLES

Turquoise cabochon

Ornamental turquoise

Turquoise in matrix

Ornamental turquoise

Turquoise stone

Group:	phosphates
Color:	sky blue, blue-green, lime green, yellow, brown
Hardness:	5–6
Cleavage:	good
Fracture:	conchoidal
Luster:	waxy to dull
Streak:	white to pale green, bluish-white
Specific gravity:	2.6–2.8
Transparency:	opaque
Crystal system:	triclinic
Uses:	jewelry; ornaments; cabochons; collectors' items; tiles

Tutankhamun's gold mask
The ancient Egyptians mined Serabit el-Khadim for turquoise. The young pharaoh Tutankhamen's funeral mask—he died in 1323 BCE—is made of solid gold, and decorated with turquoise, lapis lazuli, cornelian, quartz, obsidian, and colored glass.

Turquoise mask
This turquoise mask was made by the Aztecs of Central America. It is of the god Xiuhtecuhtli—the Turquoise Lord, God of Fire and Creator of All Life—and dates from ca.1400–1521. The turquoise mosaic is fixed on a base of *Cedrela* wood.

Sheikh Lutfollah
Built in the early 17th century, the Sheikh Lotfollah mosque in Isfahan, Iran, is remarkable for its exquisite turquoise tiles. Turquoise was also given to diplomats as presents for the rulers of other countries.

Turquoise has been **mined in Iran** for more than 2,000 years—stones from **the area** are known for their **pure color.**

Blue rain
There is a ancient legend that when Native Americans danced to celebrate the coming of the rains, their tears of joy mixed with the rain and seeped into the earth to become turquoise, the "fallen sky stone." The Navajo, Apache, and Zuni have long used turquoise for protection and healing. In more recent times, the Navajo began to produce turquoise jewelry commercially.

Turquoise sample
The name of this stone comes from the old French *turqueise* meaning "Turkish stone." It usually occurs in arid and desert regions, where groundwater seeps through alumina-rich rocks that are near copper deposits. Generally, the more copper in the makeup of the stone, the bluer the color.

JADE

SILICATE

There are two sides to jade—it was tough enough to be welded as ax heads and weapons thousands of years ago, but it is also highly prized as a beautiful gem. It was only in 1863 that a French scientist discovered that jade items from China and South America can be made from two different minerals, now called jadeite and nephrite.

Nephrite sample

The name nephrite is taken from the Greek word for "kidney," referring to the belief that nephrite was able to cure kidney disease. It is an amphibole, a variety of tremolite or actinolite, with fibrous crystals. It is more common than jadeite, and, although it is slightly softer, it is tougher because it has a denser structure.

JADE SAMPLES

Nephrite in matrix

Nephrite crystals in matrix

Rough jade crystal

Jade stone

Nephrite rock

Group: jade group

Color: light to dark green, black yellow to brown, pink, red, white

Hardness: jadeite: 6.5–7; nephrite: 6–6.5

Cleavage: good, perfect

Fracture: splintery, uneven

Luster: vitreous; dull to greasy

Streak: white

Specific gravity: jadeite: 3.30–3.38; nephrite: 2.90–3.03

Transparency: transparent to opaque

Crystal system: monoclinic

Uses: jewelry; ornaments; cabochons; carvings, collectors' items

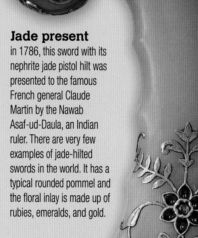

Jade present

in 1786, this sword with its nephrite jade pistol hilt was presented to the famous French general Claude Martin by the Nawab Asaf-ud-Daula, an Indian ruler. There are very few examples of jade-hilted swords in the world. It has a typical rounded pommel and the floral inlay is made up of rubies, emeralds, and gold.

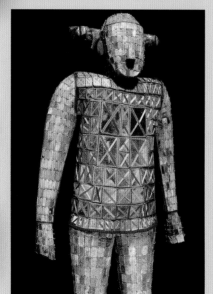

Jade burial suit

The jade burial suits of ancient China, first documented in about 320 CE, were made for royalty and were built as armor to prevent decay and keep away bad spirits in the afterlife. More than 2,000 plates of jade were threaded together with gold and silver. It is thought that it would take a skilled jadesmith at least 10 years to make one suit.

Jadeite sample

The name *jadeite* comes from the Spanish *piedra de ljada* which means "stone for the pain in the side." Spanish conquistadors observed Central Americans holding pieces of jade to their sides because they believed it could cure their problems. Jadeite is a pyroxene mineral with interlocking granular crystals.

Olmec tiger

The peoples of Central America valued jade highly and carved it into their most precious objects, including masks and statues of gods. This jade figure, probably a tiger or an ocelot, was made by a craftsman of the Olmec culture (1700–400 BCE).

Jade jewelry

Jade has been popular as jewelry for thousands of years. It is often cut into cabochons, but polished stones are also suspended from pendants, and jade beads make beautiful bracelets and necklaces. The most valuable form is imperial jade, which is an emerald green and comes from Burma.

Chinese weight

In China, jade has a history of at least 4,000 years. It was said that "a beautiful piece can be more valuable than 15 cities." Jade has been worn as jewelry, used to decorate, and carved into objects for rites of worship and burial. The Chinese even made units of weight out of jade (right).

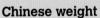

LAPIS LAZULI

LAZULITE GEMSTONE

Lapis lazuli is more stone than gem, because it is actually a rock made of many minerals. The main one (at 25–40 percent) is lazurite, which has a rich, blue color, and it is often dotted with flecks of golden pyrite. The Egyptians decorated their tombs with it, and ground it up for dramatic blue eye makeup.

Group:	silicates
Color:	various intense shades of blue
Hardness:	5–5.5
Cleavage:	indistinct
Fracture:	uneven, brittle
Luster:	dull to vitreous
Streak:	bright blue
Specific gravity:	2.4
Transparency:	translucent to opaque
Crystal system:	cubic
Uses:	jewelry; carved ornaments; cabochons; collectors' items

Jewelry
As jewelry, lapis lazuli has been valued by people for more than 6,000 years. It has been cut into cabochons, beads, and pendants like this lapis and diamond necklace.

Ultramarine
Ground lapis lazuli, used as the pigment ultramarine, makes an appearance in many famous paintings, including in the headdress in Vermeer's *Girl with a Pearl Earring*, ca.1665.

Rough lapis lazuli

Polished lapis lazuli stone

Lapis lazuli with pyrite inclusions and marble

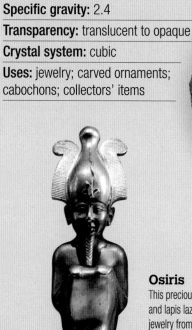

Osiris
This precious solid gold and lapis lazulli piece of jewelry from ancient Egypt (ca.1069–30 BCE) was probably hung as part of a breastplate during temple ceremonies. Osiris is crouching on a lapis lazuli pillar.

Blue rock
Lapis lazuli has been mined in northeastern Afghanistan, where this rock comes from, since 700 BCE when the country was known as Bactria. Today, the area is still the main source of this intensely blue stone.

JET
LIGNITE COAL

Jet is actually a black organic rock rather like coal (see pp.132–133), except that it is formed from trees that were washed into the sea hundreds of millions of years ago. The Romans collected it on British beaches and prized its deep black color and the way its softness allowed it to be shaped.

Group: organic gems

Color: black, brown

Hardness: 2.5

Cleavage: none

Fracture: conchoidal

Luster: velvety to waxy

Streak: black to dark brown

Specific gravity: 1.3

Transparency: opaque

Crystal system: none

Uses: jewelry; ornaments; beads; carvings; collectors' items

Jet bead necklace
When jet is polished, it takes on a deep black shine, which is where we get the phrase "jet black." It has been shaped into jet beads for necklaces and rosaries for thousands of years.

Mourning jewelry
Jet has been associated with death for hundreds of years. In 1861, Prince Albert, the much-loved husband of the English Queen Victoria, died. She was so distraught that she entered a period of mourning that lasted until her death. Black became fasionable and jet was carved into mourning jewelry, including brooches and pendants.

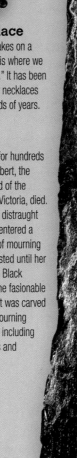

Rough jet stone

Rough jet stone

Lignite rock
Jet often has inclusions of pyrite, which give it a metallic luster. The jet of Whitby, England, is an unusually pure, hard, fossilized form of an ancient species of monkey puzzle tree that thrived in the early Jurassic era some 175–185 mya.

PEARL

CALCIUM CARBONATE

Pearls are the only gemstone made by living animals. A pearl forms when a mollusk such as an oyster or mussel finds an irritant inside its shell and coats it with the lining of its shell, called mother-of-pearl. The more layers it adds, the bigger the pearl becomes. Pearls are soft and are damaged if polished, cut, or heated.

Group: organic gems

Color: white, cream, pink, yellow, green, blue, black

Hardness: 2.5–3.5

Cleavage: none

Fracture: uneven, brittle

Luster: pearly

Streak: white

Specific gravity: 2.7

Transparency: opaque

Crystal system: amorphous

Uses: jewelry; buttons; traditional Chinese medicine; (as mother-of pearl) in cookery, as inlay for furniture and other items

Price of pearls

In 1916, the famous French jeweler Jacques Cartier bought his landmark shop on New York's Fifth Avenue. He traded two pearl necklaces for the land. Today there are more than 200 Cartier shops in 125 countries.

Pearl earrings

Early Chinese myths told of pearls that fell from the sky when dragons fought. They were thought by some cultures to be the tears of the gods. Even today, people believe that pearls bring money, protection, and luck.

Freshwater pearl

Cultured pearl

Kokichi Mikimoto

This statue commemorates the man who created the successful worldwide cultured pearl industry, which made pearls affordable and therefore available to all.

Pearl creation

Oysters and mussels produce the finest pearls of all and these natural pearls are extremely rare. Cultured pearls are grown in pearl farms. More than 10,000 pearls may be grown before a single strand of perfectly matched pearls is achieved.

CORAL

CALCIUM CARBONATE OR CONCHIOLIN

This gem is found in warm tropical waters. It is formed from the hardened skeletons of coral polyps that live in tubes on the rocky sea bed. These stones can be beautiful shades of red, white, black, or blue, although this colour can fade.

Group: organic gems

Color: white, red, pink, orange, golden, black, blue

Hardness: 3–4

Cleavage: none

Fracture: frackly

Luster: dull to vitreous, waxy

Streak: white

Specific gravity: 2.6–2.7

Transparency: translucent to opaque

Crystal system: amorphous

Uses: jewelry; cabochons; carved ornaments; collectors' items

CORAL SAMPLES

Pink coral

White coral branch

Red coral

The world's first coral reefs formed about 500 million years ago, dating back to the Cambrian period. Today many reefs are under threat from pollution and rising acidity in seawater. Red corals grow mainly in dark crevices or caverns on the seabed at depths of up to 1,000 ft (300 m) below the surface. The most desirable red corals are found in the Mediterranean and the seas off Japan.

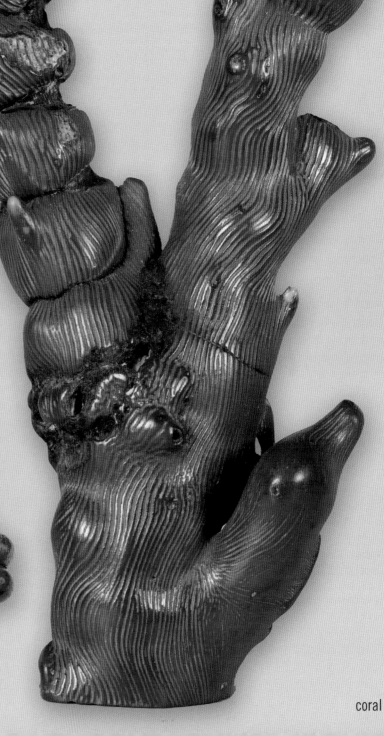

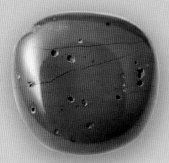

Red coral stone

Most coral gemstones are varieties of red coral. In ancient Greek legend, the hero Perseus killed the snake-headed Gorgon Medusa, and cut off her head, with which he turned his enemies to stone. While he was washing his hands, blood from the head dripped into the sea and formed red coral.

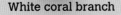

Protective coral

Throughout history, red coral has been worn to protect the wearer from storms, plague, and pestilence. The Romans hung branches around the necks of their children to ward off danger. The Gauls of western Europe often attached coral gems to their helmets and weapons to preserve themselves in battle.

Red beauty

Living white coral polyps extend from branching, antlerlike structures of red coral. This coral has a stunning bloodred color that is sought by collectors all over the world. For thousands of years, the coral skeletons have been transformed into strings of beads and other jewelry. Coral was said to protect from danger, and bring wealth and prosperity. Despite coral's central place in Mediterranean and other cultures, conservationists are now discussing how best to protect what is rapidly becoming an endangered species.

AMBER

FOSSILIZED RESIN

This organic gem is formed from a living thing, like jet and pearls are. It is fossilized sap from trees that decayed millions of years ago. The resin hardened to form a translucent, soft gem that is usually found preserved in shale or washed up on the beach. Amber amulets and pendants that date from 12,000 BCE have been found.

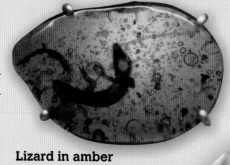

Lizard in amber
Since the first find in 1980, some rare fossilized anolis lizards in amber have been found in the Dominican Republic. Scientists have found at least five different species that lived 20 million years ago. Inside the head of one of lizard was an ant!

AMBER SAMPLES

Raw amber in matrix

Raw amber

Amber nodule

Group: organic gems

Color: yellow-orange, brownish, reddish

Hardness: 2–2.5

Cleavage: none

Fracture: conchoidal

Luster: resinous

Streak: white

Specific gravity: 1.0–1.1

Transparency: transparent to translucent

Crystal system: amorphous

Uses: jewelry; ornaments; collectors' items; building material; varnish; lacqueurs; incense; medicine

Golden stone
Most amber is cloudy and translucent, although some is completely transparent. There are two types of amber: Baltic, which is the golden yellow we associate with amber; and Dominican, which is a paler yellow.

Ancient air
The microscopic bubbles in this amber are water and gas that have been trapped there for 30 million years. By analyzing air extracted from bubbles like this, scientists have been able to establish that the air trapped inside the amber is not significantly different from the air that we breathe today.

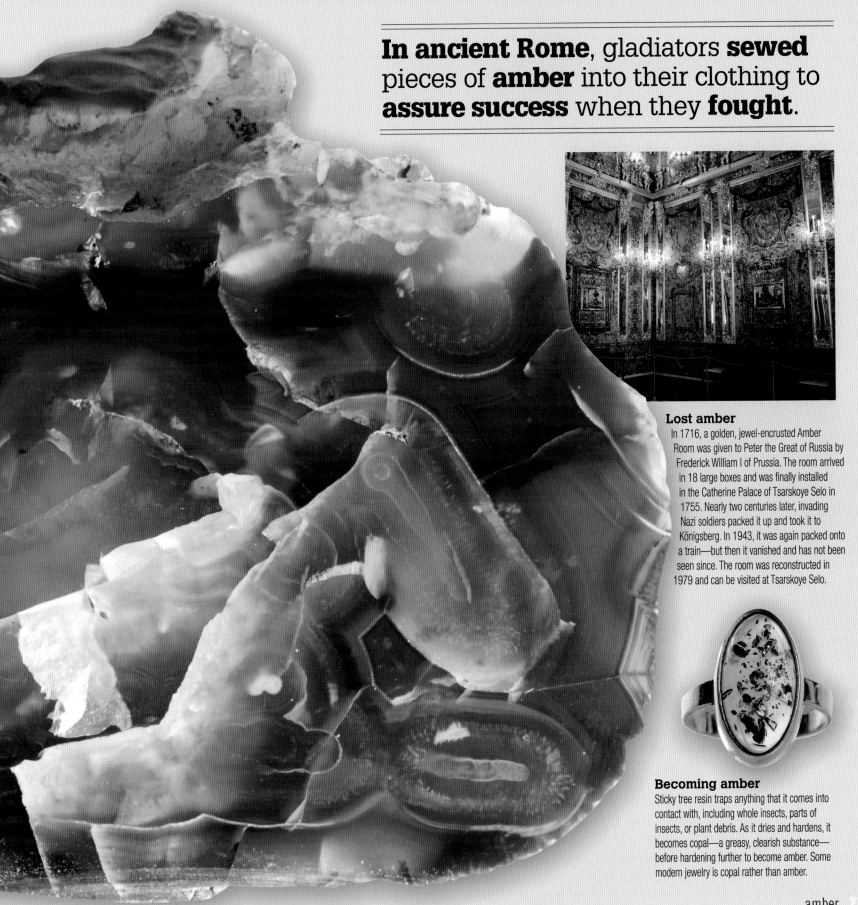

In ancient Rome, gladiators **sewed** pieces of **amber** into their clothing to **assure success** when they **fought**.

Lost amber

In 1716, a golden, jewel-encrusted Amber Room was given to Peter the Great of Russia by Frederick William I of Prussia. The room arrived in 18 large boxes and was finally installed in the Catherine Palace of Tsarskoye Selo in 1755. Nearly two centuries later, invading Nazi soldiers packed it up and took it to Königsberg. In 1943, it was again packed onto a train—but then it vanished and has not been seen since. The room was reconstructed in 1979 and can be visited at Tsarskoye Selo.

Becoming amber

Sticky tree resin traps anything that it comes into contact with, including whole insects, parts of insects, or plant debris. As it dries and hardens, it becomes copal—a greasy, clearish substance—before hardening further to become amber. Some modern jewelry is copal rather than amber.

Perfectly preserved

The fossilized remains of this insect are embedded in amber, the resin that was produced by coniferous trees that existed from the early Tertiary period, 70 million years ago. The sticky resin covered insects as it hardened, preserving their bodies. Bees, wasps, ants, flies, and mosquitoes have all been preserved in this way. This mosquito, fossilized in its amber tomb, was found at the southern end of the Baltic Sea. Baltic amber is usually found washed up on the shore with other flotsam, or it is dived for near the shoreline.

adamantine
Having a bright mineral luster, similiar to that of diamond.

aggregate
A mixture of minerals in a rock that can be separated by mechanical means.

algal
Covered in blue-green algae.

alloy
A mixture of metals, or a mixture of a metal with an element.

amorphous
Shapeless or formless; lacking a definite chemical composition.

aphanitic
Regarding a mineral: so fine grained that the crystals are not visible to the naked eye.

atom
The basic part of an element. Crystals are made up of repeating units of atoms, arranged in regular patterns. Atoms are composed of smaller particles: electrons, protons, and neutrons.

banded
Having visibly different layers.

basal
Regarding cleavage: occurring parallel to the basic crystal plane of a mineral.

batholith
An enormous volume of usually coarse- to medium-grained igneous rock that is formed when magma intrudes, or pushes its way, into a large space underground.

botryoid
A formation that resembles a bunch of grapes.

brilliant cut
A gemstone cut that is round, with triangular facets top and bottom. This cut maximizes the amount of light reflected through the top of the gem and thus increases its sparkle.

brittle
Hard, but liable to break.

cabochon
A gem that has been shaped and polished to have a smooth surface with no facets.

carat
The unit of measure used when weighing a gem. One carat is equivalent to 0.007 ounces (0.2 g).

clast
A fragment of broken rock.

cleavage
The way that certain minerals break along planes. How each breaks is dictated by its atomic structure.

clint
A section of limestone pavement.

compacted
Compressed by force. Compacting makes a mineral denser.

Post-glacier chalk conglomerate

conchoidal
With smooth, curved surfaces, like the inside of a seashell.

concretion
A rounded mass of mineral matter found in sedimentary rock.

conglomerate
Sedimentary rock that is formed from rounded gravel and boulder-size clasts that are cemented together.

corrosion
The breaking down or destruction of a material through chemical reactions.

Basalt bomb from Mount Vesuvius

crust

The outermost layer of a planet; a hardened layer, coating, or deposit on the surface of a rock.

crystal

A clear, transparent mineral; the transparent form of crystallized quartz; a solid body that has a regular shape in which plane faces intersect at definite angles, due to the regular internal structure of its atoms, ions, or molecules.

crystallize

To form crystals, often due to the evaporation of water from minerals or to a change in the temperature.

cubic

Having the form of a cube.

cushion cut

A gemstone cut that is square, but with rounded sides and corners.

cut

The process of shaping a gemstone by grinding and polishing; the shape of the final gem.

dendrite

A crystal that has a branching, treelike structure.

dike

A sheet of rock formed in a fracture in a body of pre-existing rock.

element

A substance that cannot be broken down into simpler ingredients.

extrusive

Regarding igneous rock: formed on Earth's surface from cooled lava, volcanic material, falling ash, or mudflows.

face

A flat surface on a crystal or gemstone.

facet

One cut side of a cut gem.

felsic

Regarding igneous rock: rich in light-colored silicate minerals.

fluorescence

The giving off of colored light when viewed in ultraviolet light. Materials that glow in the dark are fluorescent.

foliated

Consisting of thin, leaflike layers that can be split apart.

fossil

Any trace of an animal or plant from the past, preserved as rock. Fossils may be of bones, shells, flowers, leaves, wood, or footprints.

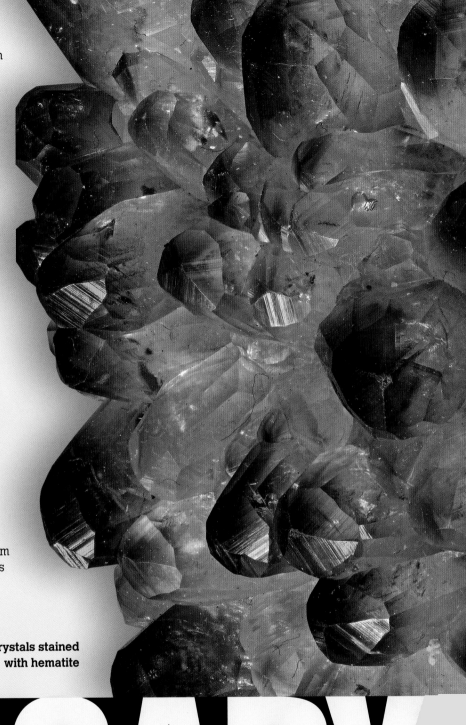

Calcite crystals stained with hematite

GLOSSARY

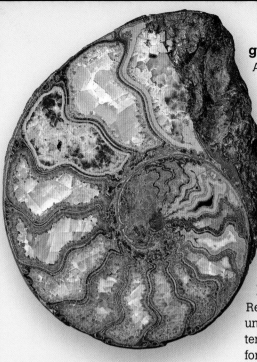

Fossilized ammonite

fracture
The chipping or breaking of a stone in a way unconnected to its cleavage planes or internal atomic structure. Fracture surfaces are usually uneven.

geode
A cavity in a rock in which crystals line the inner surface and grow toward the center.

geothermal
Relating to the internal heat of Earth.

grike
A vertical crack that forms when limestone dissolves in water and divides an exposed limestone surface into sections.

hackly
Regarding mineral fracture: having a rough surface with small protuberances.

hexagonal
Having six angles and six sides.

hydrothermal
Relating to the action of water under conditions of high temperature, especially in the formation of rocks and minerals.

inclusion
Anything that can interfere with light as it travels through a gemstone, such as a pocket of gas or air or an internal fracture.

intrusion
A body of igneous rock that invades older rock.

iridescence
The reflection of light off internal features in a gem, which produces a rainbowlike display of colors.

isometric
Having a crystal system characterized by three equal axes intersecting at right angles; having equal dimensions.

lapillus
A small stony particle ejected from a volcano. The plural of *lapillus* is *lapilli*.

lava
Molten rock that erupts at Earth's surface. Lava is called magma when it is still underground.

lithic
Relating to or composed of stone.

lithify
To change to stone or rock.

lodestone
A piece of magnetite or other naturally magnetic mineral or rock.

luster
The shine of a mineral, caused by light reflected off the surface.

mafic
Regarding rock: rich in dark magnesium and ferric compounds.

magma
Molten rock that can crystallize underground or erupt at Earth's surface as lava.

massive
Regarding a mineral: having an indefinite shape, or consisting of small crystals in masses.

matrix
The rock in which a gem is found. Also known as host or parent rock.

mesothermal
Relating to a hydrothermal mineral deposit in Earth's interior.

meteor
A rock from outer space that passes through and burns up in Earth's atmosphere. Also called a shooting star.

meteorite
A fragment of rock from outer space that reaches Earth's surface instead of completely burning up in the atmosphere.

microcrystalline
Having crystals that cannot be seen with the naked eye.

mineraloid
A mineral substance that does not have a definite chemical formula or crystal form.

monoclinic
Having a crystal system characterized by three unequal axes, with one oblique intersection.

native element
A mineral that consists of a single chemical element, not combined with other substances.

nodule
A small, irregularly rounded mass or lump of a rock, mineral, or mineral aggregate.

nugget
A small lump of gold or other precious metal.

nummulitic
Containing the shells and other debris of prehistoric sea creatures.

oolitic
Composed of concentric layers of calcite.

opalescence
A milky blue form of iridescence.

opaque
Impenetrable by light; the opposite of transparent.

ore
A metal-bearing mineral or rock that can be mined for a profit.

orthorhombic
Having a crystal system characterized by three unequal axes intersecting at right angles.

outcrop
The exposed portion of a rock formation or mineral vein that appears at the surface of Earth.

perfect
Regarding cleavage: able to split without leaving any rough surfaces.

petrified
Converted to stone or a stony substance.

phenocryst
A large crystal set into the groundmass of an igneous rock.

pigment
A coloring matter or substance.

platy
Regarding a mineral: having flat, thin crystals.

plutonic
Regarding igneous rock: solidified from magma far below Earth's surface.

polygonal
Having three or more sides, usually straight.

porous
Having small holes that allow air or liquid to pass through.

prismatic
Having parallel rectangular faces that have grown to form prisms.

Pentagonite

Porphyritic granite

GLOSSARY

Realgar crystals

pyroclastic
Consisting of material ejected by an erupting volcano.

radiation
Energy in the form of waves or rays that cannot be seen.

regional
Of or relating to a particular area or part of a country.

resinous
Having the shine of resin, a yellow or brown substance obtained from gum or the sap of some trees.

rhombohedral
Having a crystal system characterized by three equal, interchangeable axes intersecting at equal angles to one another.

rough
A rock or crystal still in its natural state, before cutting or polishing.

rough cut
A gemstone cut that has not been highly polished, so the gem still looks as if it is natural.

sediment
Material—such as silt, sand, gravel, and fossil fragments—that is transported and deposited by water, ice, or wind. Sediment forms in layers on Earth's surface. Sedimentary rock is consolidated sediment.

silica
A crystalline compound that is abundant as quartz, sand, and many other minerals.

silt
Earthy matter or fine sand carried by water and deposited as sediment.

stalactite
A long, thin deposit of carbonate minerals, hanging from the roof of a cave.

stalagmite
A tall, thin deposit of carbonate minerals, rising from the floor of a cave.

streak
The color of a mineral or gemstone when it is ground to a powder.

synthetic
Regarding a stone: made in a laboratory, but having the same chemical composition, crystal structure, and physical and optical properties as a natural stone.

tarnish
To dull the luster of a surface.

toxic
Containing poisonous substances.

translucent
Semitransparent.

transparent
See-through, clear, or crystalline.

trigonal
Shaped like a triangle.

twinned crystals
Paired mineral crystals that grow together.

Tektite

ultraviolet
Relating to rays of light that cannot be seen. Ultraviolet radiation has wavelengths that are slightly shorter than wavelengths of visible light and longer than those of X-rays.

vein
A thin sheet of minerals that fills a crack or fracture in a rock.

vesicle
A small cavity in volcanic rock that was formed by gas trapped inside the lava.

vitreous
Regarding a gem: having a glasslike shine and reflecting less than 30 percent of the light that falls on it.

vitric
Resembling glass.

xenolith
A rock fragment that becomes enveloped when a large igneous rock hardens around it.

GLOSSARY

A

aa lava 90
abrasives 44, 56, 60, 68, 102, 122, 136, 160, 176, 184, 188, 194, 196
adamite 51
agate 51, 64, 158, 174–175
aircraft 25, 52
albite 44, 168
alchemists 189
alkali feldspars 44, 45
alloys 47, 48, 53, 81, 162
    see also steel
almandine 11, 138, 160
aluminum 52, 68–69, 81
amazonite 51
amber 159, 210–211
amethyst 176, 180–181
ametrine 159, 182
ammonite 65, 120
amphibolite 154
andalusite 152
andesine 44
anglesite 9, 55
animals, navigation 61
anorthite 44, 45
anorthoclase 44

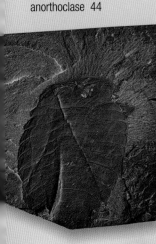

anthracite 24, 132, 135
apatite 96
aquamarine 97, 158, 159, 162, 168–169
aragonite 17, 51
arsenic 84, 85, 87
arsenopyrite 51, 84–87
ash, volcanic 90, 94, 101
Aspidorhynchus 121
Australia 33, 109, 184–185, 187
aventurine 139, 176
azurite 22

B

barite 9, 17, 78–79, 111
barium 44, 78, 79
basalt 90, 91, 94–95, 98, 154–155
batholiths 11, 92, 97
batteries 24, 34, 55, 80, 97
bauxite 68–69
benitoite 78
bentonite 36
beryl 13, 97, 159, 162–163, 164, 167, 168
beryllium 163
biotite schist 11, 138
birds 61, 183, 192
bituminous coal 132
bixbite 162, 163
blackboards 117, 149
bloodstone 176
blue john 70, 71
boehmite 68, 69
bolivianite 182
boracite 50, 67

borax 66–67
brachiopod 120
breccia 111, 118, 131
brochantite 16
Bronze Age 19
bulletproof vests 67
Burgess shale 110, 119, 121
bytownite 44, 45

C

cadmium 81
calcic skarn 139
calcite 9, 17, 50, 74–77, 113, 116, 126, 140
calcium carbonate 74–77, 113, 116, 126
Canada 110, 119, 121, 145, 167
carbon, graphite 24–25
carbonates 9, 22–23, 74–77, 112–113, 116, 126
carbon fiber 25
carnelian 64, 159, 176
cars 24, 26, 27, 34, 55, 162
catalytic converters 26
cave paintings 59, 117
caves 59, 75, 114–115, 116, 117, 154
celestite 111
cell phones 16, 28
celsian 44
cement/concrete 36, 60, 68, 74, 112, 113, 116, 119, 129
ceramics 37, 44, 46, 54, 70, 84, 128, 136, 184

Burgess shale with
***Sidneyia* fossil**

Boracite with orange
hilgardite crystals

INDEX

cerussite 17, 51
chalcedony 9, 17, 64–65, 174, 177
chalcopyrite 18, 22
chalk 116–117, 131
chert 11, 130, 136
China 37, 38–39, 171, 175
china pottery 36–37, 44
chondrite meteorite 41, 42
chromite 52–53
chromium 53
cinnabar 17, 82–83
circuit boards 32, 35, 192
citrine 159, 177, 182–183
clay minerals 36–37, 59, 119, 130
cleavelandite 50, 158, 171
cliffs 116, 117, 146, 152
clints 112
coal 24, 56, 111, 131, 132–135
cobalt 17
coccoliths 117
colemanite 67
columbite 96
computers 25, 28, 32, 162
conductors 18, 32, 34, 35
conglomerate 11, 110, 111, 118, 130
cooking utensils 18, 28–29, 36–37, 69
copper 17, 18–19, 110
copper carbonate 22–23
coprolite 120
coral 77, 158, 207–209
corundum 60, 161, 192
cosmetics 54. 68, 80, 85, 103, 132, 140
crocoite 53
crown jewels 193, 195

crystal structure 8, 9
cuprite 18, 20–21, 22
currency 18, 27, 34, 35, 81

D
Delft pottery 37
desert rose 111, 129
detergents 66, 67
diabase 90, 91, 109
diamond 13, 155, 158, 191, 196–199
diaspore 68, 69
diatomite 130
dikes 11, 97, 171
dinosaurs 74, 120, 121, 175
diopside 140
dioptase 17, 51
diorite 91
dolerite 90, 109
dolomite 17, 83, 131, 171
dragonfly 121
dravite tourmaline 170

E
earthquakes/tsunamis 163
Easter Island 101
echinoids 11, 120, 121, 130, 136
eclogite 155
Egypt, ancient 23, 32, 41, 54, 59, 93, 123, 137, 145, 146, 164, 170, 189
elbaite 170
electricity 18, 32, 34, 132, 148, 171

electronics 16, 18, 35, 80, 96, 176
elements 14
emerald 13, 53, 162, 164–167, 191
epidote 50, 154
evaporites 128, 129

F
feldspar 16, 44–45, 108, 145, 194
fertilizers 36, 60, 116
fingerprints 25
fireworks 69
flint 110, 111, 130, 136–137
flowstones 75
fluorescent minerals 46, 48, 49, 70–71, 80, 194

fluorite 9, 17, 50, 51, 70–73, 84
fool's gold 30–31
forsterite 40
fossil fuels 133
fossils 65, 74, 94, 110, 112–113, 117, 119, 120–121, 130, 149, 175
fulgurite 147

G
gabbro 90, 91, 108
galena 9, 34, 54–57
gallium 81
galvanization 81
garnet 140, 144, 154, 155, 159, 160–161, 190

gems 12–13, 158–213
geodes 174, 180–181, 182, 183
gibbsite 68, 69
gilbertite 96
glacial till 131
glass 44, 52, 66, 70, 78, 104–105, 112, 123, 147, 176, 192
glendonite 74
gneiss 91, 123, 138, 145, 171
goethite 17
gold 14, 16, 32–33, 49, 146
goshenite 162, 163
granite 11, 90, 91, 92–93, 96, 110, 171, 173, 188
graphene 25
graphite 17, 24–25
Greece, ancient 141, 180
grikes 112
grossularite 160, 161
grossular marble 140
gypsum 9, 17, 110, 111, 129, 131
gyrolite 51

H
hagstone 137
halides, fluorite 70–71
halite 110, 128, 130
halloysite 36
heat 25, 34, 66, 132
helictites 75
heliodor 159, 162
heliotrope 176
hematite 9, 28, 50–51, 58–59, 74, 78, 80
herbicides 66
hessonite garnet 161
hilgardite 50, 51
hornblende 154
hornfels 138, 139, 152–153
hyalophane 44
hydrofluoric acid 70
hydrothermal deposits 57, 78, 83, 91
hydroxides, bauxite 68–69

Fluorite

Orpiment

I

igneous rocks 90–109
  basalt 94–95
  dolerite 90, 109
  gabbro 108
  granite 92–93
  obsidian 104–107
  pegmatite 96–97
  pumice 102–103
  tuff 100–101
ignimbrite 100
India 47, 141, 165,
  194, 196
insecticides 84, 144
iridium 81
iron 16, 17, 24, 28–29,
  30–31, 42–43, 58–59,
  60–61, 62–63, 70, 74,
  81, 112, 116, 120, 131
Italy 101, 103, 113, 141

J

jade 165, 202–203
jasper 64, 111, 177
jaspilite 139
jet 158, 205

K

kaolinite 36
kernite 67
kimberlite 155, 199
kukersite 130
kyanite 8, 144,
  145, 155

L

labradorite 44,
  158, 159
lapilli, pumice 103
lapis lazuli 13, 190, 204

lasers 48, 162, 194
laterite 36
lava 90, 94, 102, 104
lead 16, 54–55
leather 53, 84
lenses 70, 71, 169
Leonardo da Vinci 181
lightning 147
lignite 111, 132
limestone 110, 112–115,
  131, 140, 171
limonite 18, 28
lithium 97, 128
lodestone 61

M

magnesium 40–41, 69
magnetite 28, 50, 60–63
magnets 26, 28, 47,
  60–61, 63
malachite 17, 22–23
marble 11, 138, 139,
  140–143, 154
marcasite 9, 55, 116
marl 111, 122
marmatite 73
Mars 45, 58, 59, 113
masks 19, 23, 27, 83,
  93, 105
medicine 26, 28, 32, 34, 46,
  55, 66, 74, 79, 80, 81,
  83, 84, 85, 97, 102, 104,
  132, 165, 175
megalodon 121
melnikovite 87
mercury 83
metallic elements 14,
  18–19, 26–27, 28–29,
  32–33, 34–35, 54
metalworking 19, 35, 49, 56

metamorphic rocks 138–155
  amphibolite 154
  contact
    metamorphism 153
  eclogite 155
  fulgurite 147
  gneiss 91, 145
  hornfels 138, 139,
    152–153
  marble 140–143
  quartzite 146
  schist 144
  slate 119, 139, 148–151
meteorites 11, 42–43
  coal impact 131, 132
  Martian 45, 113
  olivine 41, 43
  tektites 147
Mexico
  Aztec calendar stone 95
  Aztec emeralds 165
  Aztec knife 65, 104
  Aztec mask 105
  Mayan mask 23
  Mayan pyramid 113
mica 50, 91, 110, 138,
  140, 148
microcline 44, 45
migmatite 11, 139
minerals 8–9, 14–87
mining 35, 133–
  135, 184, 197
molybdenum 49
monticellite 40
Moon 26
moonstones 44

Fluorite

INDEX

morganite 159, 162
motorcycles 53
muscovite 49, 96

N

nacrite 36
Napoleon 69, 193
native elements 18, 24–25,
   26, 28–29, 32, 34–35,
   196–199
navigation 61, 162, 168
New York 92, 113, 122
New Zealand 33
Noah's Ark 160
noble metal 26
nuclear radiation 34, 47, 48,
   54, 55, 58, 60, 67, 78
nuggets, gold 12, 32

O

obsidian 11, 91, 104–107
octopus 18
oil and gas industry 78, 133
oil shale 119, 130
oligoclase 44, 45
olivine 40–41, 45, 90, 108
opal 13, 184–187, 190

orpiment 84
orthoclase 44, 45
oxides 9, 58–59, 60–61,
   192–193, 194–195

P

paint 23, 44, 59, 60, 68,
   74, 78, 80, 83, 84, 117,
   136, 140
palladium 26
panning for gold 32
paper 66, 74, 78, 129, 140
pavements
   limestone 112
   slate 150–151
pearl 206
pegmatite 96–97, 171,
   173, 188
pencil lead 16, 24
pens, ballpoint 96
peridot 40, 159, 164
petalite 96
petrification 65, 121, 127
pezzottaite 163
phosphorite 130
photography 35, 60, 71
pipes 18, 36, 55
pitchstone 104
plagioclase feldspar 44, 45,
   52, 90, 91, 108, 154
plaster 129

plastics 70, 74, 78,
   80, 132
platinum 26–27, 81
poison 84, 85, 87
Pompeii 101
porcelain 37, 44, 46, 128
pottery 37, 44, 54,
   70, 119
powellite 49
pumice 90, 102–103
pyrargyrite 34
pyrite 16, 17, 28, 30–
   31, 120
pyroclastic rock 102
pyromorphite 16
pyrope 160
pyrophyllite 36, 96
pyroxene 41, 45, 140, 155

Q

quartz 9, 32, 50, 56–57,
   64–65, 91, 158, 159,
   173, 176–183, 188,
   190, 191
quartzite 122, 138,
   139, 146

R

radar 162
radio, crystal 55
realgar 9, 17, 50, 84
rhodochrosite 191
rhyolite 90, 188
rock crystal 176
rock gypsum 17, 110,
   111, 129
rock rose 65

rocks 10–11, 88–157
   dating 46
rock salt 110, 128, 130
Romans 55, 71, 103, 127,
   132, 148, 169
rose quartz 158, 176,
   177, 191
royalty, and gems 193,
   195, 197
rubber 44, 78, 80, 102
ruby 13, 53, 158, 161, 191,
   194–195
Russia 23, 98–99, 188, 189
rutile 63, 192

S

salt, rock 110, 128, 130
sand 129, 147, 176
sandstone 11, 110, 111,
   122–125, 130–131, 146
sanidine 44, 45
sapphire 159, 161, 190,
   191, 192–193
scheelite 48–49
schist 11, 138, 139,
   144, 171
schorl 170
scolecite 51
scoria 91, 103
seals, hematite 59
sea pen 120
sea urchin 11, 120, 121,
   130, 136
sedimentary rocks 110–137
   breccia 118
   chalk 116–117
   coal 132–135
   flint 136–137
   limestone 112–115
   rock gypsum 129

rock salt 128
sandstone 122–125
shale 119
tufa 126–127
semiconductors 54,
   176, 192
serpentinite 52, 138
shale 10, 110, 119, 121,
   122, 130
shellfish 61, 81, 77, 110,
   116, 120, 121
silicates 9, 35–37, 40–41,
   44–45, 46–47, 64–65,
   162–163, 168–169,
   174–175, 176–179,
   180–181, 184–187,
   188–189
silver 16, 34–35
sinkholes 118
skarn, calcic 139
slate 119, 139,
   148–151
soap 80, 102,
   128, 132

sodium chloride 128
South Africa 33
South America 33, 128,
   142–143, 165, 181, 188,
   189, 192
space 32, 49, 55, 58,
   59, 66, 69, 94, 95, 160,
   163, 197
   see also meteorites
spark plugs 27
specularite 51
spessartite 160, 161
sphalerite 17, 57, 73,
   80–81
spherulitic obsidian 104
spinels 52–53, 195

Tufa

**Brown
vesuvianite
crystals
with calcite**

spodumene 97
stalactites 23, 75, 126, 130
stalagmites 75, 114–115, 126
staurolite 144, 145
steel 24, 28, 29, 47, 48, 52–53, 60, 70, 116, 132
stibnite 51
Stonehenge 109
stony meteorite 41, 42, 43
sulfates, barite 78–79
sulfides 54–57, 80–81, 82–83, 84–85
sunstone 44, 158

T

Taj Mahal 141
teeth 61, 121
tektite 11, 147
terra-cotta 37, 38–39
tigereye 65, 177, 191
tillite 118
tincalconite 66
titanium 63, 69
tools 18, 49, 137
topaz 97, 159, 169, 188–189, 190

tourmaline 12, 13, 50, 91, 97, 158, 167, 170–173
toys, metal 28, 81
travertine 126
trilobite 120, 149
tsavorite 161
tsunami prediction 163
tufa 11, 126–127
tuff 91, 100–101, 111
tungstates, scheelite 48–49
tungsten 48, 96
turquoise 13, 191, 200–201

U

ulexite 67
ultraviolet light 46, 48, 70–71, 194
uvarovite 160, 161

V

vanadinite 17
vayrynenite 96
Venus 55
vermiculite 36
vesicular basalt 94, 103
Vesuvius, Mount 101, 103
vivianite 9
volcanic rock
basalt 94–95, 98–99
obsidian 104–107
pumice 102–103
tuff 100–101

W

Wales, slate 148, 149
Washington 113, 141, 145
watch movements 161, 176, 192, 194
water
purification 68, 132
repellants 132
softeners 67, 128
watermelon tourmaline 12, 158, 170
weapons 19, 137
weather forecasting 163
wolframite 48
wood, petrified 121
wrought iron 29

X Y

xenolith 11, 90, 101, 199
xylophone, hornfels 153

Z

zinc 80, 81
zircon 13, 16, 46–47
zirconium 47

Vesicular lava

INDEX

Photographs ©: 123RF: 158 center right (Aleksandras Naryshkin), 180 center right (alessandro0770), 183 center right (Alexey Sokolov), 12-13 bottom, 158 center right bottom, 174 left center top, 174 left center top, 182 left center bottom, 182 left bottom (Anastasia Tsarskaya), 161 top left, 161 top left far top, 161 right top, 168 left top, 168 left center top, 182 left center top, 184 left center top, 188 left center bottom (Andy Koehler), 159 center left top (Ansis Klucis), 210 right, 211 left (Artem Povarov), 185 center right (Christian Wei), 161 right center top, 190 center right (dipressionist), 184 center right (Fritz Hiersche), 177 bottom left (Gontar Valeriy), 75 top center (gozzoli), 184 left center bottom (Heinz Meis), 90 bottom left (hydognik), 90 center bottom (joannawnuk), 75 center (Joshua Haviv), 90 right, 91 left, 139 top left (Kjetil Dahle), 185 top right (Krzysztof Wiktor), 206 right bottom (Laurent Renault), 182 left center (madlien), 65 top center (marigranula), 184 left center (Michael Gray), 78 left bottom (missisya), 158 center bottom (Nika Lerman), 204 right center (Oliver Mohr), 210 left center (pawelproc), 202 left center (Penchan Pumila), 202 left center bottom (Phalakon Jaisangat), 24 left bottom (photographieundmehr), 47 bottom right green, 47 bottom right pink (Ratchapol Yindeesuk), 160 bottom right, 161 bottom left (rozaliya), 68 left center bottom, 90 center top, 91 top left, 91 center bottom left, 91 center bottom right, 91 center right, 138 center left, 138 center right top, 138 bottom center right, 138 bottom right, 139 center left top, 139 center right top (Slim Sepp), 162 left center top (stellargems), 70 left bottom, 161 right bottom (Terry Davis), 174 left center bottom (vangert), 203 center right (Viktoriya Chursina), 23 center left (Vladislav Gajic), 36 right, 37 left, 65 center, 74 left center top, 139 center, 139 center right top, 139 bottom center, 158 center, 158 center right top, 159 top right bottom, 170 left center, 182 left top, 188 bottom center, 200 left center, 207 bottom left (vvoennyy), 178-179 (Wang Song), 184 center left (Zbynek Burival), 185 bottom right (Анна Павлова), 171 top center, 191 center right (Михаил Приманов), 171 center right top (Михаил Примаков); Alamy Images: 49 top left (42pix), 67 right top (Alan Curtis), 132 top right (All Canada Photos), 19 bottom right (Ancient Art & Architecture Collection Ltd), 83 top left (Basement Stock), 49 top center, 49 right top (blickwinkel), 33 bottom right (Chris Howes/Wild Places), 136 right, 137 left (Christian Hütter), 53 bottom right (Corbin17), 137 top right (Darkened Studio), 201 bottom right (David South), 120 center top (Gabbro), 48 bottom right, 49 bottom left (Gary Cook), 183 center left (Greg C Grace), 105 bottom right, 193 center left (Heritage Image Partnership Ltd), 126 bottom center (Images & Stories), 53 top left (Jacob Halls), 97 bottom center (Jeremy Pembrey), 180 center left (john angerson), 52 left bottom, 68 right, 69 left, 137 center top (John Cancalosi), 154 bottom left (Karel Tupý), 101 center left (Mary Evans Picture Library), 203 top right (Miss Sarah Steele), 163 bottom right (MPAK), 194 top center (North Wind Picture Archives), 176 bottom center (Oxfordshire Photography Project), 19 center left top (Peter Horree), 52 left center top, 105 center bottom (PjrStudio), 146 top left (PRISMA ARCHIVO), 140 bottom center (Ryan McGehee), 193 center right (Serbia Pictures: Adam Radosavljevic), 153 top left (Slim Sepp), 37 bottom right (Simon Curtis), 71 bottom right (StockPhotosArt - Technology), 49 right center top, 53 center right (Susan E. Degginger), 93 center right top, 202 bottom center left (The Art Archive), 52 bottom right, 53 bottom left, 71 center right (The Natural History Museum), 145 top left (The Print Collection), 206 center left (Tomas Abad), 104 top center (trekandshoot), 26 left bottom (Universal Images Group North America LLC/DeAgostini), 205 center left (Valery Voennyy), 61 center right (View Stock), 170 top right (WENN Ltd), 183 top center (Westend61 GmbH), 26 left center right (WILDLIFE GmbH), 208, 209 (Wolfgang Pölzer), 83 center top, 195 top right, 201 top left (World History Archive); Bigstock/stocktributor: 101 center right; Chris Pellant: 92 bottom left, 97 top center right, 116 bottom left, 145 bottom left; Corbis Images: 169 bottom right; Dreamstime: 121 bottom right (Abraham Badenhorst), 127 top right (Aiisha), 207 center bottom (Alexander Potapov), 174 bottom center (Andrea Hornackova), 200 left center (Anusron62), 207 center top (Apolobay), 211 top right (Aschaefer85), 164 bottom left (Ashwin Kharidehal Abhirama), 117 bottom right (Aspenphoto), 204 bottom left (Bo Li), 81 center right (Boltenkoff), 83 top right (Brett Critchley), 192 bottom center (Carlo Ferraro), 165 bottom right (Chaopavit), 204 top left (Chelsie Ritter), 123 top center (Chuanwentao), 19 center (Chuyu), 170 bottom center (Constantin Opris), 168 bottom center (Danilo Mongiello), 82-83 bottom left (Danolsen), 194 left bottom (Dario Lo Presti), 103 center top (Dimasobko), 75 bottom center (Dragoneye), 127

Aragonite

center right (Duffloop), 180 right, 181 left (eanyu), 204 right bottom (Epitavi), 111 bottom left (Evgeny Dontsov), 29 bottom left (Evgeny Karandaev), 40 left center bottom (Farbled), 29 top right (Fisechko), 148 bottom left (Gail Johnson), 102 bottom left (Galyna Andrushko), 197 top right (Gary Arbach), 202 left center bottom (Gennady Gorobets), 144 top center (Ginasanders), 202 left top (Goldminer), 168 left center, 194 left center top (Gozzoli), 25 bottom right (Grzegorz Kieca), 55 top center (Ian Poole), cover top center right, 4 bottom left, 200 left bottom (Igor Kaliuzhny), 210 left top (Iluzia), 97 bottom right, 192 left bottom, 192 left center bottom (Ingemar Magnusson), 69 top right (Irochka), 200 left center top (Ismael Tato Rodriguez), 181 bottom right (Jakub Krechowicz), 206 center left (Jens Tobiska), 146 bottom left (Joe Ferrer), 75 top right (Jsmcqueen), 41 center right bottom (Karol Kozlowski), 206 bottom center (Kasia Biel), 37 center top, 137 center top right, 137 center bottom (Ken Backer), 174 left center bottom (Kenny Tong), 165 top center (Kettaphoto), 122 center center top (Kittidech Inkhotchasan), 200 bottom center (Kivandam), 134-135 (Kodym), 35 center left (Ksena2009), 37 top right (Lai Ching Yuen), 206 top left (Lenanet), 132 bottom left (Linda Bair), 145 top center (Louis Henault), 180 left center top (Luis Carlos Torres), 95 top right (Marina Pissarova), 180 left bottom (Mario Bonotto), 19 top right (Mark Eaton), 165 center right (Mark Watson), 117 top center (Matthew Ragen), 175 center right (Mgkuijpers), 111 top center left (Michal Baranski), 180 left center bottom, 181 top right (Milahelp S.r.o.), 136 center center top, 175 top left, 188 left bottom (Mrreporter), 194 bottom center (Murali Nath), 70 top right (Nastya22), 81 top center (Nathan Clifford), 29 center left (Nebojsa Babic), 177 bottom center left (Nikkytok), 19 bottom center (Nikolai Sorokin), 69 center right (Nikshor), 196 bottom center (Nila Newsom), 122 bottom left (Nylakatara2013), 144 bottom left (Oleksandr Khalimonov), 37 center right (Patricia Hofmeester), 25 top left (Paul Cowan), 149 center right (Paul Fleet), 28 left center top (Paul Moore), 160 bottom left (Philcold), 79 top right (Pleprakaymas), 169 top right (Rainer Walter Schmied), 109 bottom left (Robert Paul Van Beets), 155 top center (Rozaliya), 29 center top (Scphoto48), 29 bottom left (Serban Enache), 169 center right top (Serge75), 130 bottom center (Slim Sepp), 189 top center (Siloto), 194 right, 195 left (Stephan Pietzko), 211 bottom right (Stevieuk), 141 center right (Studiomixov), 123 top left (Swissmargrit), 168 left center center bottom (Tatiana Morozova), 78 top (Thomas Lenne), 177 top right (Unholyvault), 189 bottom center (Venusangel), 75 center right (Victor Gomez), 180 left center (Vlad3563), 207 bottom center (Vvoevale), 147 bottom left top (Walter Kopplinger), 174 right, 175 left (Wojciech Tchorzewski), 177 center right bottom (Yury Kosourov), 204 top center (Zerbor), 38-39 (Zhongchao Liu), 122 top right (Zhukovsky); Eberhard Frey, Helmut Tischlinger/PLoS One: 121 bottom center; Fotolia: 128 bottom left (aaron_huang86), 201 top right (acmanley), 55 bottom left (Al), 129 center (aleks-p), 121 center right (alice_photo), 164 center (andy koehler), 32 right, 33 left (Artur Marciniec), 176 left center top (baldomir), 110 bottom left (Becky Stares), 184 left bottom (Björn Wylezich), cover spine bottom (borissos), 133 bottom right (bozhdb), 101 bottom center (Bryan Busovicki), 98-99 (budkov), 119 center left (carlosvelayos), 67 top center (cataliseur30), 119 bottom left (chendri887), 133 center right (cherniyvg), 49 center right top (ChiccoDodiFC), 112 bottom left (chris2766), 81 center (Claudio Divizia), 97 top left (dessauer), 141 top right (Dimitri Surkov), 59 center right bottom (Dmitry Pichugin), 113 bottom right (doncon402), 103 bottom right (DPM75), 176 left bottom (Edith Ochs), 97 top center left (ejnelson314), 93 top right (eugenesergeev), 34 left bottom, 132 center bottom (farbled_01), 129 bottom left (Fyle), 133 bottom center (Georg Lehnerer), 52 top right frame (goir), 25 center bottom (Guan Jianchi), 22 top bottom (Gudellaphoto), 113 top right (H.Peter), 23 bottom center (ID1974), 47 center bottom (Igor Kali), 22 left bottom, 55 right center top (jarous), 35 center top (Jeffrey Daly), cover spine bottom center, 177 bottom right (joannap), 37 top left (Josemaria Toscano), 61 bottom center (Kerry Werry), 28 left center bottom, 28 left bottom (Kletr), 176 left center (Konstantin Milenin), 123 top right (Lars-Ove Jonsson), 25 center right (Laurentiu Iordache), 61 top center (leisuretime70), cover left center bottom (Lubos Chlubny), 128 center top, 129 center top, 190 bottom center, 191 center right top (marcel), 121 center bottom (markrhiggins), 110 center top (michal812), 22 right, 23 left (mindelio), 64 left center top (Mivr), 149 center left (Nathalie Landot), 129 center bottom (NoraDoa), 41 center right top (Olga Khoroshunova), 40 right, 41 left (Only Fabrizio), 33 gold nuggets (pani_yana), 113 center top (Patryk Kosmider), 194 center left (pbombaert), 83 bottom right (philip kinsey), 111 bottom right (prima91), 161 center left (rauf_ashrafov), 141 top left (refresh(PIX), 141 bottom right (robert cicchetti), 93 center bottom (Ross C), 40 left top, 176 left center bottom (S_E), 94 bottom left, 118 right bottom, 119 right center, 131 top center right, 131 top right, 131 bottom left, 132 center center top, 132 bottom right, 133 left (slimsepp), 112 top right, 121 top left (Sora), 95 bottom right (spumador), 100 bottom center (Stefano Gasparotto), 177 center (stellar), 113 center bottom (Studio Barcelona), 81 top right (susan orton-flynn), 111 center right bottom, 128 center bottom (Swapan), 35 top center (sytilin), 105 top right (Tarzhanova), 35 bottom left (tommypic), 59 top center (Tristan3D), 111 center right top (Tyler Boyes), 28 right, 29 left (uwimages), 113 center right (VanderWolf Images), 22 left top (vangert), 29 center right (vichie81), 122 center center bottom, 136 center, 138 center right bottom, 139 center right bottom, 139 bottom right top, 139 bottom left top, 140 left far bottom, 176 left top, 177 bottom center right top, 177 center right top (vvoe), 164 center bottom (W.Scott), 149 bottom right (yossarian6); Gary Ombler: 202 bottom center right; Getty Images: 42 right, 43 left (Boyer), 53 top right (Dave King), 152 top right (De Agostini Picture Library), 59 bottom right (De Agostini/A. Dagli Orti), 27 top right, 85 center right top, 97 center right (DEA/A. Dagli Orti), 47 top right (DEA/G. Cigolini), 52 top right (DEA/M. Carrieri), 48 top right (DEA/R. Appiani), 126 left top (Dorling Kindersley), 42 top right (Edward Kinsman), 175 bottom center (Fotosearch), 26 left top, 26 right, 27 left (Harry Taylor), 23 bottom right (Janet Schwartz), 66, 67 bottom left (John Cancalosi), 155 bottom left (Leroy Francis), 49 right bottom (Mark A Schneider), 193 bottom center (Max Mumby/Indigo), 193 top right (Patrick Kovarik), 23 top right (Print Collector), 40 top right (Ron Dahlquist/Design Pics), 55 top right (Science & Society Picture Library), 85 bottom right (Sergio Anelli/Electa/Mondadori Portfolio), 49 bottom right (Stephen Saks), 65 top right (Universal History Archive), 171 center (UniversalImagesGroups), 41 top right (Werner Forman), 52 left center bottom (Yashuhide Fumoto); iRocks.com/Rob Lavinsky/Wikimedia: 67 right center bottom; iStockphoto: 120 bottom right, 121 bottom left (angi71), 120 center right bottom (BruceBlock), 120 bottom left (Crazytang), 55 center bottom (Ensup), 136 center bottom (ffolas), 110 center

far left, 130 top center right (Gala_Kan), 18 left top (hapelena), back cover top fifth from right (ikonacolor), 109 bottom right (jessicaphoto), 141 center left (kanvag), 93 bottom center (karimhesham), 128 top center (merial), 117 center right (nobiggie), 127 bottom right (panopticum), 108 bottom left (Peeter Viisimaa), 162 center bottom right (PhilipCacka), 155 top left (ProArtWork), 162 left bottom (Reimphoto), back cover top far right (selensergen), back cover top third from left (SunChan), 110 center right bottom (VvoeVale); LegendsOfAmerica.com: 67 center bottom; Library of Congress: 33 center right (Keystone View Company), 33 top right; Lyle Gordon, Northwestern University: 61 bottom right; Michael Till, Gloucester/www.michaeltill.com: 153 top right; NASA: 47 top left (GSFC/METI/ERSDAC/JAROS/U.S./Japan ASTER Science Team), 103 top right (Jesse Allen, NASA Earth Observatory/MODIS Rapid Response System, Goddard Space Flight Center), 55 top left, 55 center left, 95 bottom center (JPL), 197 center right (JPL-Caltech/R. Hunt (SSC)), 69 center left, 113 top left, 160 top right, 163 center left, 163 center right; National Park Service/Yellowstone National Park: 104 bottom left; Science Source: 25 center top (Andre Geim & Kostya Novoselov), 30, 31 (ANT Photo Library), 124, 125 (Art Wolfe), 67 right center top, 67 right bottom (Ben Johnson), 56, 57, 60 left bottom (Biophoto Associates), 121 center right top (Biophoto Associates/Mary Martin), 126 left center top (Biophoto Associates/Robin Treadwell), 18 bottom center (British Antarctic Survey), 203 bottom right (Clive Streeter/Dorling Kindersley/Science Museum, London), 71 top right, 196 left top (Colin Keates/Dorling Kindersley/Natural History Museum, London), 60 left center bottom, 78 left bottom center (De Agostini Picture Library), 72, 73 (De Agostini/C. Bevilacqua), 41 bottom right, 42 bottom left, 42 top right, 42 top center, 42 bottom center, 43 center top, 43 center right top (Detlev Van Ravenswaay), cover bottom center right (Dirk Wiersma), 44 top right, 64 bottom center, 76, 77, 108 top center, 127 center, 146 top center, 172, 173, 202 left center top (Dirk Wiersma), cover left center, 210 left bottom (Dorling Kindersley), 118 center (Dr. Carleton Ray), 42 center bottom (Dr. Morley Read), 196 left bottom (E. R. Degginger), 67 center top (Editorial Image), 121 center top (Francois Gohier), 169 center right bottom (Gary Ombler/Dorling Kindersley), 43 top center right (Gary Ombler/Dorling Kindersley/Oxford University Museum of Natural History), 133 top right (H. Armstrong Roberts/ClassicStock), 36 left top, 36 left center bottom, 36 left center top, 45 right top, 45 right center top, 45 right bottom, 45 right far bottom, 49 right center top, 52 left top, 64 left center bottom, 64 left bottom, 116 center top, 170 left top, 170 center, 203 top center, 205 bottom left, 205 right top, 205 right bottom (Harry Taylor/Dorling Kindersley), 18 left center top, 83 center bottom (Harry Taylor/Dorling Kindersley/Natural History Museum, London), 54 (Hermann Eisenbeiss), 121 right (Javier Trueba/MSF), 189 top right (Jean-Loup Charmet), 165 top right (Jeff Rotman), 20, 21, 34 left top, 44 center, 46 left gemstones, 58 left far top, 58 left bottom, 61 top, 68 left bottom, 80 top right, 165 center left, 198, 199 (Joel Arem), 210 bottom left (John Koivula), 142, 143 (John Shaw), 42 center left, 109 center center bottom, 109 center center top (Joyce Photographics), 147 center top (Kent Wood), 32 left top, 45 right far top (Linda Burgess/Dorling Kindersley), cover bottom left, cover spine top, 46 top right, 46 bottom right, 47 bottom left, 70 left center top, 83 right center, 180 left top, 191 center (Mark A. Schneider), 43 top right (Mark Williamson), 149 bottom center (Martin Bond), 79 top left (Mary Martin), 43 top center left, 45 top center (Massimo Brega), 18 left center, 62, 63 (Michael Szoenyi), 43 bottom right, 186, 187 (Millard H. Sharp), cover right center top (Natural History Museum, London), 210 top center (Noah Poritz), 32 left center (Paolo Koch), cover top center, 121 center left top (Pascal Goetgheluck), 67 bottom right, 197 bottom right (Patrick Landmann), 44 bottom right, 45 left, 97 top right, 165 center top (Phil Degginger), 55 right bottom, 65 bottom right (Phil Degginger/Jack Clark Collection), 25 top right (Philippe Psaila), 32 bottom left (Photo Researchers, Inc.), 161 top center (Power and Syred), 158 center bottom left (Raul Gonzalez Perez), 196 left center bottom (RIA Novosti), 41 top center, 68 left top, 158 bottom center right, 191 center right bottom (Richard Leeney/Dorling Kindersley), 114, 115 (Robbie Shone), 189 bottom right (Roberto de Gugliemo), 49 center left (Russell Lappa), 68 left center top (Science Stock), 86, 87, 120 top left (Sinclair Stammers), 42 center top, 43 center right bottom, 47 center top, 81 bottom right, 163 top right (SPL), 166, 167 (Stephen J. Krasemann), 117 top right (Steve Gschmeissner), 147 center bottom, 175 bottom right, 207 right (Ted Kinsman), 35 top right (Theodore Clutter), 32 left center bottom (Tom McHugh), cover left center top, 67 top left, 206 right top, 212, 213 (Vaughan Fleming), 55 bottom center (Will & Deni McIntyre), 85 top center (Zephyr), 35 bottom right, 59 center right top, 85 center right bottom, 95 center right; Shutterstock, Inc.: 34 right, 35 left, 55 right center, 75 bottom right, 194 left center bottom (Albert Russ), 136 bottom left (Alexey Kamenskiy), 27 center right (AlexLMX), 93 center top (BasPhoto), 19 top left (bogdan ionescu), 23 top center (Dimedrol68), 2-3 bottom (Enlightened Media), 36 left bottom (farbled), 162 left top (Jarous), 26 bottom center (Jeffrey B. Banke), 22 left center (Jiri Vaclavek), 162 left center bottom (Karol Kozlowski), 110 top center left (kavring), 152 bottom left (M Andy), 101 top right (Morphart Creation), 171 top left (Ondrej Prosicky), 110 center bottom (papa1266), 22 left center bottom (Pi-Lens), 37 center left (pixs4u), 150-151 (Sigur), 177 center left (spectrumblue), 106-107 (Tami Freed), 105 top center (verbaska), 36 left center, 100 left center bottom, 110 center, 111 top left top, 111 top center right (woe), 18 left center bottom, 24 left top, 28 left top, 110 bottom right, 130 center left top, 130 center left bottom left, 130 center left bottom right, 131 center, 131 center right, 131 bottom left bottom (www.sandatlas.org), 27 bottom right (You can more); Thinkstock/MarcelC: 55 top right; USGS: 161 right center bottom.

All other images © Scholastic Inc.

The publisher would like to give particular thanks to the following people for their help: Ali Scrivens, John Goldsmid, Marybeth Kavanagh, Debbie Kurosz, and Ed Kasche; Dr. Wendy Kirk, Dr. Adrian Jones, and curator Nick Booth of University College Museums and Collections, London; Peter and Judith Briscoe, Steetley Minerals, Nottinghamshire, England; Sam Lloyd, Estelle Deschamps, and Rachel Stubberfield of Holts, London; and Michael Till, Gloucester, England, www.michaeltill.com.

ACKNOWLEDGMENTS